MW01126674

HOW TO START A SUCCESSFUL CANDLE-MAKING BUSINESS

QUIT YOUR DAY JOB AND EARN FULL-TIME INCOME
ON AUTOPILOT WITH A PROFITABLE CANDLE-
MAKING BUSINESS—EVEN IF YOU ARE AN ABSOLUTE
BEGINNER

HENRIETTA SMITH AND WALTER GRANT

© **Copyright 2022 - All rights reserved.**

The content contained within this book may not be reproduced, duplicated or transmitted without direct written permission from the author or the publisher.

Under no circumstances will any blame or legal responsibility be held against the publisher, or author, for any damages, reparation, or monetary loss due to the information contained within this book, either directly or indirectly.

Legal Notice:

This book is copyright protected. It is only for personal use. You cannot amend, distribute, sell, use, quote or paraphrase any part, or the content within this book, without the consent of the author or publisher.

Disclaimer Notice:

Please note the information contained within this document is for educational and entertainment purposes only. All effort has been executed to present accurate, up to date, reliable, complete information. No warranties of any kind are declared or implied. Readers acknowledge that the author is not engaged in the rendering of legal, financial, medical or professional advice. The content within this book has been derived from various sources. Please consult a licensed professional before attempting any techniques outlined in this book.

By reading this document, the reader agrees that under no circumstances is the author responsible for any losses, direct or indirect, that are incurred as a result of the use of the information contained within this document, including, but not limited to, errors, omissions, or inaccuracies.

CONTENTS

INTRODUCTION

Thousands of candles can be lit from a single candle; Happiness never decreases by being shared.

— BUDDHA

Emma –30– had worked as an administrative assistant at a law firm for five years. She was married with one kid and planned to have more kids shortly. However, she struggled with balancing her personal and professional life as her job was quite demanding. She didn't have much time to relax with her family, let alone engage in hobbies.

When the pandemic hit, she was forced to work from home most of the time. This was good news because it meant she could spend more time with her daughter and her husband, as well as find time for her new hobby—candle making. Emma's love for candles began while her daughter was still in preschool when she would give handmade candles out as gifts to her daughter's school teachers. She got great feedback on her creations and decided to try a candle-making business on a part-time basis.

Her hobby, now turned into a business, caused her to bring in a whopping $2,000 per month, within the first three months of selling candles. From then onward, Emma quit her job and turned her hobby into a full-blown business. In just two years, she has created a six-figure candle-making brand and ships her beautiful products across the world.

There might be several parts to Emma's story that you can relate to. For one, you might be living a busy lifestyle, trying desperately to manage your work-life balance. You might feel pressure to work harder and look for additional income streams to support your fast-growing family. Or perhaps you are someone who is interested in entrepreneurship and dreams of working from home. However, due to time constraints and a lack of proper research, you haven't been able to sit down and think about a potential business idea and what it would take to start a profitable business.

Regardless of your motivation, you have chosen to pick up this book and learn about the art and business of candle-making. You've made an excellent choice because according to the National Candle Association (2020), you are entering an industry that grosses $3.2 billion per year. Not only is the industry good for profits, but it's also become a cultural phenomenon! It's estimated that 7 out of 10 American house-holds use candles as part of their home decor. This isn't hard to believe because what's not to love about quality aromatic candles (bonus points if they are handmade and sourced locally)?

Like any other business, starting and running a successful candle-making business requires an investment of time, money, and sheer hard work. However, what you invest into starting your business doesn't compare to the lifelong perks that come with it, like finally getting to quit your day job and being a full-time boss, or having the option of expanding your business so you can build an international brand! What's more, is that you don't need a degree in finance or entrepreneurship to get started. Heck, you don't even need to lease an office space or purchase heavy equipment. All you will need is this manual, a clean workspace, and a few handy supplies and tools to get started!

And who are the experts guiding you along your candle-making journey?

Henrietta Smith is a successful American entrepreneur who specializes in the candle-making business. She has always had an entrepreneurial spirit, ever since she played with dolls as a little girl and combined creativity with an appreciation for beauty. When she was just 12 years old, she asked her mother to teach her how to sew so she could make dresses for dolls. She then sold these dresses to her classmates and neighbors and soon became popular among her peers.

After graduating from college, Henrietta set aside her business endeavors and tried her luck as a nurse. However, she soon realized that she wasn't happy with what she was doing and eventually went back to her first love—making and selling beautiful things that bring happiness to others. During that time, she had engaged in candle-making as a hobby and decided to turn that into a business. Unlike her first venture, her candle-making business was not an immediate success. Despite producing beautiful and fragrant candles, she was not selling as many as she hoped. In fact, the first time she joined a craft fair, she only sold two candles.

But Henrietta is not the type who would let a few hitches dampen her spirit. Learning from her mistakes, she made sure to research the market extensively before trying again. Her determination, passion, and openness to learning soon paid off. Today, Henrietta is an expert in the candle-making business and has expanded her line to candle accessories, as well as scents and soaps.

Our second expert, Walter Grant, is an American entrepreneur and business author. As a child, Walter was considered a creative type and was often seen to be "in his own world." He kept designing the most unique creations with the materials he found lying around the house. That creative spirit never left him, and after university, he knew he wanted to go into entre-preneurship. However, his dream did not come to fruition as easily or quickly as he thought. After his graduation, Walter landed a corporate job and worked there for five years, until one day he decided to quit.

He took the leap of faith and went out on his own and started his own business. After two years of hard work, the business still hadn't taken off as he first expected and he had to file for bankruptcy. Even though this was a major setback, he did not quit. After a short break, he got back on his feet and decided to start from zero. This time, after learning from his previous mistakes, he made quick progress, and after a few years, moved on to selling his second company for multiple eight-figures.

The dynamic duo has written this book to help aspiring entrepreneurs turn their passion into profits and build a successful candle-making business. They have been through the highs and lows of starting a new venture and hope that with their expertise in their respective fields, they can provide proper guidance to those who seek to escape the corporate 9-to-5 and become their own boss.

After reading this book from cover to cover, you will walk away knowing how to set up your business, produce quality handmade candles, and market your products to the right customers. Are you ready to learn the art of candle-making and the business behind it?

Your journey to a seven-figure business begins right now!

PART I

IGNITE YOUR PASSION:

LEARNING THE BASICS OF CANDLE-MAKING

1

WHY YOU SHOULD START A CANDLE-MAKING BUSINESS

In this chapter, you will learn:

- The background of the candle-making industry.
- The simple business model for starting your candle-making business.
- The opportunities and challenges of running a candle-making business.

A QUICK GLIMPSE AT THE STATS

There are probably many reasons why you are interested in starting a candle-making business, but one of your biggest motivations is making a profit! After all, you are an entrepreneur (or an aspiring one at that) and your primary objective is making money.

Fortunately for you, the candle-making industry is a prospering one, and it doesn't seem to be showing any signs of slowing down. The candle manufacturing market is projected to grow by 5.26% each year, from 2021 to 2028, reaching %10.66 billion by 2028 (Verified Market Research, 2022). One of the biggest opportunities for growth in this market is the use of paraffin wax in producing candles, which customers see as an environmentally-friendly option, as opposed to plastic candles. The National Candle Association predicts that more than a billion pounds of wax is used in the U.S. annually to manufacture different types and scents of candles.

Candles are typically sold in gift shops, department stores, grocery stores and drug store chains. However, increasingly, more start-up entrepreneurs are entering the space and producing and selling their homemade candles online. According to WaxMelters, there are over 400 commercial candle manufacturers in the U.S. who operate either on a small or large scale and produce candles for at home or commercial use. With numerous shapes, sizes, and fragrance options (approximately 10,000 different candle scents to be exact), businesses have a lot of room to be creative and come up with unique products. The more novel the candle, the higher it sells for, but retail prices generally range between $1.99 for a small prayer candle to $35 for candles that come in pillars or jars.

What makes candles in demand are the various ways they can be used. Market research carried out by WaxMelters found that 9 out of 10 consumers use candles as part of their home décor to make a room feel comfortable. The preferred spaces within a home to burn candles were the living room (42%), kitchen

(18%), and bedroom (13%) (WaxMelters, n.d.). Both men and women agreed that candles were the perfect gift for a range of occasions, like a birthday present, housewarming gift, festival gift, or dinner party gift.

As good as it is to hear the benefits for consumers, you might be wondering what's in it for you. First, let's discuss how much it will cost you to start a candle-making business. While start-up costs will be different for each business, you can expect to invest between $1,000-$1,700 in start-up capital. And since production costs of making candles are so low, you can expect to make a profit margin of 30%-75% on a candle. For instance, if it costs you $5 to make a candle, you can easily add a margin of 50% and charge your customers $10 for the candle. With this kind of setup, you would need to sell 200 candles to make $1,000 per month.

With so many ways to customize candles, there is a gap for your candle-making business in this fast-growing industry. You deserve to get your share of the profits and turn your hobby into a seven-figure business!

IS CANDLE-MAKING THE RIGHT BUSINESS FOR YOU?

Being passionate about candles can get one foot in the door, but the success of your business depends on whether this type of business is the right fit for you. Like any kind of business, the candle-making business comes with its risks and rewards which you need to take time and think about. Here are a few opportunities and challenges of starting and running a successful candle-making business:

Opportunities

Besides making a lot of money and having the flexibility to work from home, here are some of the other opportunities you are afforded when you start a candle-making business

- **You can structure your business the way you like.** You get to decide how small or large you want your business to be, the kinds of candles you produce, and the ideal customers you target. You can also decide whether to serve a local market or open your business to an international market.
- **You can turn a passion into a career.** If you are a creative person who enjoys doing crafts, you can make money out of your beautiful creations. Working on something you care about can feel rewarding and make the hard work of starting your business feel worth it.
- **You can save money on start-up costs.** You don't need an office or retail store to start your candle-making business. A clean workspace at home and a few tools and supplies to make your candles will do. You also have the option of selling your candles online, which means you get to reduce your start-up and operating expenses significantly.
- **It's easy to attract customers.** Since consumers have a natural love for candles, you can encourage impulse buying by creating promotions, offering discounts, or

advertising themed candles during certain holidays or festivals.

- **There is a high likelihood of referrals.** If your candles look amazing and smell even better, there is a high chance that you will receive referrals. Of course, having a structured referral program will boost your chances even more and create an incentive for your customers to tell their friends and family about your products.

Challenges

Despite the opportunities presented, the candle-making business can come with its unique challenges

- **There is high competition.** Whenever the market is booming, you can expect a lot of tough competition. It's important to conduct a thorough market analysis before you start so you can identify where there is a demand.
- **The trouble of finding the right supplier.** Many businesses in this industry prefer to find a supplier who can take care of the production side of things. However, finding the best supplier can take a lot of time and energy. You can save yourself the hassle by setting up your small production space at home and making your own candles.
- **Lack of worker benefits.** Unlike being employed, when you are starting up your own candle-making business, you will be responsible for the majority of the tasks, like production, sales, marketing, and managing your

finances. You will need to cover your own insurance, pay your taxes, and find a way to secure your business online. You will also need to ensure that your business is stable and generating enough money before you can pay yourself a monthly salary.

- **Producing candles can feel repetitive.** Since you will start by selling one type of product—candles—you may start to feel tired of the same repetitive candle-making process. The trick is to diversify your product ranges so you have enough room to be creative.
- **Building a loyal customer base can be difficult.** If you are planning on selling your candles online, you will have limited face-to-face interactions with customers. This can make it difficult to build relationships with your customers and encourage repeat business. You will need to go the extra mile in creating an appealing brand and being responsive to your customers' needs.

Now that you have a good idea of the kind of market you are entering, the next step is learning about the components of a candle!

2

KNOW YOUR CANDLE: WAX, WICKS, AND EVERYTHING IN BETWEEN

In this chapter, you will learn:

- The key components of a candle—wax and wicks.
- Different types of candle wax.
- Elements that give candles their X-Factor, such as color and fragrance.

ALL ABOUT WAX

When you think of a beautiful wax candle, what image comes to mind? Are you reminded of the white candles placed on candlestick holders at church? Or the aromatic candles you burn in your living room? Over the years, candles have become more sophisticated. About 3,000 years ago, in Ancient Egypt, candles didn't look as good as they do today.

The Egyptians made candles called rushlights that were used for religious celebrations. Rushlights were made by soaking the core of the rush plant in melted animal fat or grease. They got the job done and were also affordable to produce, although they didn't have a wick. The Romans are recorded in his history as being the first to produce what we know today as wicked candles. How did they come up with this genius invention? They wrapped a roll of papyrus (from the papyrus plant) around twine and repeatedly dipped the twine into a mixture of beef or mutton fat, known as tallow. Compared to rushlights, these wicked candles lasted longer and were refined over centuries to become the candles we know and love today!

Modern-day candles are composed mainly of two elements: wax and the wick. Apart from using different types of those elements, what makes candles different from each other are the colors and fragrances. In this section, we will learn more about wax and the different types you can use to make your candles.

Wax is a combustible substance made of either animal, vegetable, or petroleum components. When it is heated above room temperature, it melts and takes a liquid form. You can think of wax as the source of fuel for a candle, but in order for the fuel to burn, the wick must be lit. Burning the wick is what kick starts the process of lighting a candle. The flame will stay alight for as long as the wick absorbs the liquid wax. However, during this process, all you notice is the pleasant scent filling every corner of the room. The scent continues to circulate throughout the room, until the flame is put out.

Different Types of Wax

1. Paraffin Wax

There are many types of wax to choose from in the market. One of the most popular types of wax is paraffin wax. The reason manufacturers love this type of wax is because it holds fragrances well and releases a strong scent. However, paraffin is made from petroleum, a fossil fuel that releases a lot of energy when burned, which makes it a non-renewable and unsustainable resource. Moreover, there is research suggesting that burning paraffin can release harmful cancer-causing toxins in the air. However, research pointing out the health hazards presented by burning paraffin has been refuted by organizations like the European Candle Association.

Since customers are leaning toward sustainability and environmentally-friendly products, there are a few alternative types of waxes that are in high demand. Below are just a few.

2. Soy Wax

Soy wax is a type of vegetable wax made from soybean oil. The process of making soybean oil begins by harvesting, cleaning, cracking, then rolling soybeans into flakes. The oil is extracted from the soybean flakes and goes through a hydrogenation process, where unsaturated fatty acids found in the oil are saturated. This ensures that the oil can solidify at room temperature and liquefy when burned above room temperature.

Candle manufacturers enjoy working with soy wax because it is an environmentally-friendly product, compared to paraffin wax. Soybeans are a natural resource and therefore biodegradable. Soy wax also burns slower than other wax forms, which means that the candle generally lasts longer. The only downside is that soy wax doesn't hold fragrance well as compared to other types of wax, meaning that your candle will likely release a subtle scent.

3. Beeswax

Beeswax has been around since the Middle Ages and is loved for how it burns cleaner and doesn't release a smokey flame. Beeswax is a natural material that is secreted by the worker bees in a colony. Beeswax candles aren't made of pure beeswax since it has a pungent sweet scent that can interfere with the candle's fragrance. Since beeswax is naturally tough, it can cause tunneling, a phenomenon where only a small portion of the wax burns, particularly around the wick, making a pool of liquid wax within hours of being lit.

Beeswax is best used as a complementary wax combined with softer wax like coconut or soy wax, so the candle can hold a good shape and retain longer-lasting fragrance. Beeswax is environmentally-friendly and has been found to purify the air of dust and other air pollutants. However, consumers who follow a vegan lifestyle are likely to stay clear of beeswax and opt for a more vegan-friendly product.

4. Coconut Wax

Coconut wax is the latest type of wax offered in the market. It is made by extracting coconut oil from coconut meat. The coconut oil is then cleaned and filtered, creating a completely biodegradable wax. It can be expensive to get your hands on coconut wax, however, the major selling points are that it burns clean and is a sustainable material. Be mindful that if you want to make coconut wax candles, you will need to add another hardening wax in your formula since coconut wax is very soft and won't be able to hold a lot of fragrance.

5. Rapeseed Wax

Another new player in the market is rapeseed wax, also known as Canola Wax. Rapeseed oil is made from extracting the oil that comes out of the rapeseed plant after harvesting. Candle manufacturers love it because it can burn for longer and retains fragrance really well. Similar to coconut wax, it is natural and sustainable, and it is increasingly becoming more popular than soy wax.

The type of wax you use depends on several factors. For instance, you might have a personal preference for one type of wax than another or the target audience you are appealing to may have their own wax preference. Another factor to consider is how much you are willing to spend on wax and what type of candle you are seeking to make. If you want your candles to hold a certain shape or burn well in certain containers, then going for harder waxes might be the best approach. You also might want to consider how strong you want the fragrance of your candles to be, or how long you want your candles to burn. Take your time to weigh the advantages and disadvantages of each type of wax to determine one that is suitable for your products.

ALL ABOUT WICKS

The main function of a wick in a candle is to deliver the liquid wax to the flame so that the candle can burn and release a pleasant aroma. The wick is made up of small fibers that are bundled together to make it easier to absorb the liquid wax. You can think of the candle wick as the heart of the candle that keeps the flame alive.

There are two phenomena that you must avoid when choosing the right wicks for your candles: being under-wicked or being over-wicked. When you are under-wicked, your wick size is too small for the candle, which means that your candle won't burn out to the edge of your candle container, but will instead burn down and create a tunnel. Another common problem you might experience when you are under-wicked is not being able to sustain the flame.

You should also avoid being over-wicked meaning that your wick size is too large for your candle. You will be able to tell because the flame will be large in comparison to your candle and it will also flicker continuously. Since the flame is large, you will also notice that your melt pool (liquid wax) is deeper than 1/2 inch and your wick is releasing too much carbon, causing a black mark or stain at the tip (a process known as mushrooming). So far, we understand that the size of the wick is important and it can influence the flame size, burn rate, melt pool, tunneling, or mushrooming. However, other factors that can affect your choice of wick include

- Type of wax
- Wax melting point
- Candle size (particularly the diameter of the candle or container)
- Color and fragrance materials
- Shape of the candle

Different Types of Wicks

There are generally four different types of wicks you can choose from; however, each of the four types of wicks can have different cores and other unique characteristics—making the options endless! The four types of wicks are

1. Flat Wicks

Flat wicks are made of small fibers that are braided together. They are the most common type of wick in the market and work well for pillar and taper candles and other freestanding candles. Flat wicks are self-trimming, which means that they curl up after burning and won't create a large flame.

2. Cored Wicks

Cored wicks contain another material within the braided fibers of the wicks. This core material can be zinc, cotton, or paper. The core material helps the wick stand tall, without compromising its form while burning. Due to the sturdy nature of these wicks, they are recommended for use in pillar and container candles.

Cored wicks are popular in the market for the sturdiness and aesthetic they can bring to a candle. In the U.S. candle manufacturers typically use cotton or cotton paper as a core material in their wicks; however, other varieties include metal or wooden wicks.

3. Square Wicks

Square wicks have square tips with rounded edges, which makes them more robust than flat wicks. They are often used in beeswax candles but can work well when used in pillar or taper candles too.

4. Specialty Wicks

Specialty wicks are custom made to match the burn characteristics of special candles like oil lamps or outdoor candles.

FRAGRANCES AND COLORANTS

There isn't much room for creativity when it comes to choosing the right wax and wicks, however, you have a lot of room to get your creative juices flowing when selecting the fragrances and colorants you will use for your candles.

Adding fragrance to a candle isn't mandatory, although in the U.S. market it can enhance the overall quality of a candle. In fact, the National Candle Association estimates that about 75-80% of candles sold in the U.S. are scented (National Candle Association, 2014).

Choosing the right fragrance isn't merely about what smells good, but also about what can burn well too. There are over 2,000 natural and synthetic fragrance materials to choose from which are made from essential oils or synthetic fragrance chemicals. These fragrances are safe, made of the best quality, and are compatible with different types of wax.

The endless choice continues when selecting colorants for your candles. Here, you can be as imaginative as you want to be, creating your own combination of colors, mixing colors, or creating metallic, pastel, or rich shades. Consumer psychology shows that consumers expect the color of a candle to match the perception of the fragrance. For example, if a customer is purchasing a "Fresh Ocean Breeze" candle, they expect the color palette to mirror the colors often found near the ocean, like shades of blue, beige, and white.

The color of a candle is achieved by playing with dyes and pigments. Dyes are used to create special color effects and can help you achieve your perfect shade. They give candles their translucent color, and the best part is that they don't interfere with the candle's burn rate. Pigments have the same effect as paint. They coat a candle with color and are therefore used on the outside of a candle. Unlike dyes, the color of pigments don't bleed or fade, so you can expect your solid color to remain throughout the life of your candle.

Both dyes and pigments are safe to use on candles and according to the National candle Association, there are no known health hazards that either cause.

Now that you are knowledgeable about the basic elements of a candle, it's time to discuss the different types of candles to help you determine which is a good fit for your business.

3

KNOW YOUR CANDLE: DIFFERENT TYPES OF CANDLES

In this chapter, you will learn:

- The different types of candles available on the market.
- Simple step-by-step guidelines on how to make each type of candle.

THE CAVEAT FOR CHOOSING THE PERFECT TYPE OF CANDLE

There is no right or wrong way of choosing the type of candles you seek to use for your business. However, the only factor that could influence your decision is the kind of use you have in mind for your candles.

Take a moment and think about the types of candles you know of. You may not know them by their names, but you could've seen them in specific places, like at home or at a festival.

Depending on how you imagine your candles to be used and enjoyed, you will need to select a certain type of candle.

For example, if you imagine customers burning one of your scented candles while enjoying a relaxing soak in the bathtub, you would need to consider selling pillar or glass candles. But if you imagine customers burning your candles at special functions or dinner parties, you would do well-selling votives or floating candles.

Therefore, before you continue any further, reflect on how you imagine your candles being used. This will help you narrow your options when considering the various types of candles.

TYPES OF CANDLES AND HOW TO MAKE THEM

You are familiar with the basic elements of a candle, but wax, wicks, fragrance, and color can be fashioned in different shapes and sizes. With your desired candle use in mind, here is a list of the main types of candles and practical steps on how to make each candle at home:

Container Candles

Container candles are popular and perhaps the easiest to make at home. The scented and colored candle wax is poured into a container made of any kind of candle-safe material like wood or glass and left to set. Here are the steps for making a container candle

Materials needed:

- Cooking pot
- Wax
- Wick
- Fragrance
- Dye
- Mixing utensils

Step 1: Choose Your Wax, Wick, and Container

Prepare your chosen wax, wick, and container. If you haven't decided on a type of wax or wick, you can refer to chapter 2. Make sure that your chosen wax isn't too soft or too hard and that your chosen wick is proportionate to the kind of container used. You have a lot of room to play around when selecting your container. Depending on the aesthetic you are trying to achieve, you can choose a regular mason jar, teacup, candle-safe bowl, or different shapes of glassware. Have a browse on the internet and see what creative ways other candle-makers have used containers.

Step 2: Choose Your Fragrance and Color

You are welcome to make scentless and colorless candles if that is what appeals to your audience. But generally speaking, many customers prefer scented and colored candles. If you are knowledgeable about essential oils, pick some of your favorites and create candles with that particular scent. Alternatively, you can combine a few synthetic candle-making oils and come up with your custom scents. You can also decide on a scent based on the time of year. For example, for a winter range of candles, you can play around with woody, spicy, and musky scents and for a summer range you can play around with floral scents. Some scents are appropriate all year round like vanilla or linen.

Choosing your fragrance first can help you decide on the color of your candle. Buy a range of candle-making dyes and either go with a color most suitable for the scent or enjoy the process of creating your own shades.

Step 3: Prepare Your Wick and Wax

Since you are making your candle at home, you will also need to prepare your wick at home. The first step is to decide how long you want your wick to be. Ensure that you are not over-wicked or under-wicked by cutting the twine at least three inches longer than the length of your container. Don't worry about making your wick too long because you can always cut to size later on.

Put your wick aside and get started on melting your wax. Place solid wax into a heat-resistant bowl and place over a pot of boiling water. Bring the heat to 170°F - 180°F; make sure it doesn't reach boiling point. Once melted, add the fragrance and dye you have chosen to the liquid wax. Stir until it reaches an even and liquid consistency. Reduce the heat so that your wax doesn't boil.

Once you have melted your wax, submerge your twine into the melted wax for a minute. Use a pair of kitchen tongs to avoid getting hot wax on your hands. Remove the twine from the wax and hang it up to dry, making sure that it is hanging completely straight.

Step 4: Fix Wick and Wax Into Container

When the wick is dry, place it inside the middle of the container. You can either suspend it with a string or hold it straight with your tongs. Next, pour your melted wax evenly into the container. The pouring temperature of your wax should be between 150°F-160°F for best results. Continue firmly holding down the wick as you pour your wax, until the candle sets. Once the candle is set and has solidified, you can trim your wick to the perfect size. And there you have it—a beautiful container candle!

Pillar Candles

Pillar candles are molded candles that stand upright without any support. The wax is usually thick and deep enough to burn on a heat-resistant plate without falling apart. If the candle is wicked the proper way, it can burn evenly without making any wax spills on the plate. Here are simple steps on how to make your own pillar candles at home

Materials needed:

- Cooking pot

- Wax
- Wick
- Fragrance
- Dye
- Thermometer
- Candle mold
- Plate
- Utensils

Step 1: Choose Your Wax and Wick

When choosing your wax, keep in mind that you will need a strong enough material to hold the candle firm. If you want to use softer waxes like soy wax, make sure you purchase one that is specifically made for pillar candles. Blended wax consisting of different types of wax can also help you achieve firmness while holding scent really well. When choosing the wick, it is generally recommended to use a flat or braided wick.

Step 2: Choose Your Fragrance and Color

You have a lot of options to choose from when picking the right fragrance and color. When measuring how much fragrance to use for your pillars, a general rule of thumb is to add an ounce of fragrance for every pound of wax. Play around with different dyes to achieve custom colors, or go the minimalist route and use a single color.

Step 3: Prepare Your Mold

To set your pillar candles, you will need to purchase a candle mold. Fortunately, candle molds come in all sorts of shapes and sizes, giving you a wide variety to choose from. You can also pick your mold based on the type of material, such as aluminum or polycarbonate molds. Aluminum molds work best when you are making standard round, square, or oval pillar candles, whereas polycarbonate molds allow you to make custom geometric shapes, plus they enhance the glossy outside texture of your candles.

Before pouring melted wax inside your mold, preheat the mold so that your hot wax doesn't set unevenly and cause you not to achieve a consistent and smooth finish on your candles.

Step 4: Prepare Your Wax

Place solid wax into a heat-resistant bowl and place it over a pot of boiling water. Bring the heat to 170°F-180°F and make sure it doesn't reach boiling point. Add your fragrance and colorant into your pot and stir until you achieve consistency. The pouring temperature of your wax should be between 150°F-160°F for best results. You can also pour your fragrance just before pouring your wax into the mold to avoid over-heating your fragrance (this can change the chemical compounds of your fragrance).

Step 5: Pour and Cool Wax

Fix your mold on a plate and insert your wick. Thereafter, pour your melted wax inside the mold. Leave enough space in your mold for a re-pour of wax once your wax has cooled. In general, your pillar candles will need a re-pour for a smooth quality finish. Wait an hour or two for your wax to cool at room temperature before your re-pour. Waiting more than two hours can lead to wax shrinkage. You will need to wait for another hour or two to remove the mold from your candle after your re-pour.

Votive Candles

Votive candles are a cross between a container candle and a pillar candle. In most cases, the candle comes separately from its votive container. When you are ready to burn the candle, you insert it inside the container and it melts to fill the shape of the container. Therefore, to make a votive candle, you can follow the same guidelines for making a pillar candle.

Dipped Candles

If you are a lover of all things artistic, then dipped candles may just be the right product for you! As the name suggests, you dip a long twine of the wick into melted wax, repeatedly, until the outer layer thickens and takes the form of a candle. You can choose to dip the wick in the same colored wax or mix things up and create a multi-colored candle. Here are the steps on how to make your own dipped candles at home

Materials needed:

- Crockpot
- Wax
- Wick
- Fragrance
- Dye
- Utensils
- Cup

Step 1: Melt Your Wax

To make your beautiful dipped candles, you can use beeswax or any other non-petroleum based wax. Drop chunks of wax into a large crockpot and put the stove on low heat. Wait for your wax to melt, but make sure it doesn't start boiling.

Step 2: Prepare Your Wick

When measuring the length of your wick, you will need to first estimate the depth of your melted wax. Ideally, your wick should be double the depth of your wax, plus a few extra inches so your fingers can grab onto it.

Step 3: Start the Dipping Process

Fill an old drinking cup with cold water and place it next to your crockpot. Pick up your wick and hold it with two fingers in the middle. Straighten both ends before dipping them into your melted wax as deep as you like, and quickly bring it up again. Immediately dip your wax-coated wick into the cold water and use your fingers to straighten the wick so that no curves are running along with your candle. Repeat this process (dipping the wick in wax and immediately steeping it in water) until you achieve the kind of thickness you desire. If you plan on placing your dipped candle in a candle holder, be mindful of your candle size and thickness.

Step 4: Let Your Candle Cool

When you have achieved the correct size and thickness, hang them on a portable indoor rack or kitchen towel rack. Once dry, you can trim your wicks and store your candles indefinitely.

Rolled Candles

Rolled candles are made from soft sheets of wax that are rolled to form a pillar. The most common wax used to make rolled candles is beeswax due to how soft and pliable it is. Beeswax also adds a warm yellow glow in any space and carries a sweet subtle scent. Here are the steps for making rolled candles at home

Materials needed:

- Beeswax sheets (either 8-inch or 16-inch sheets)
- Primed wick (dipped in melted wax and dried)
- Sharp knife or razor
- A suitable workspace

Step 1: Cut the Wick

Lay out the beeswax in front of you and gently place the wick along its side. Make sure the wick is 3/4 quarters longer than the sheet of wax. It's recommended to leave 3/4 inches on either side of the wax sheet. This will give you the freedom to choose which side of the rolled candle will be the top or the bottom later on.

Step 2: Roll the Candle

Lay the wick on the edge of the sheet of wax and start rolling the sheet, first enclosing the wicks, and then bending the wax to form a roll. Continue bending the wax until you reach the other side. As you bend, keep your roll tight around the wick. It's also important to keep your roll of wax even. Keep an eye on both ends and ensure your candle is straight. For added thickness, you can add another sheet of wax to your candle. When you have rolled the first sheet, take a second sheet and run it along the edge of the first one. Press both sheets together firmly so that they merge. Then, continue rolling as usual.

Step 3: Complete Rolling

After you have finished rolling your last sheet of wax, gently press down the edge of the wax sheet until you achieve a smooth edge. If you left 3/4 inches of wick on both ends, choose which end looks neater and make it the top of your candle. Trim the wicks from the bottom completely and reduce the wick from the top to 1/2 inch.

After having learned how to make five types of candles at home, which type of candle are you most interested in making?

After learning about the different types of candles, it's time to know more about the tools used to make them.

4

BUILD YOUR CANDLE-MAKING SPACE AND TOOLBOX

In this chapter, you will learn:

- The type of tools and equipment that are essential in the candle-making business.

FROM KITCHEN COUNTERTOP TO BASEMENT WORKSHOP

When Emma began her candle-making business, she would find a corner in her kitchen and make that her workspace. Her kids would constantly complain about how her candles were taking up *all* of the prep space and her husband who is a "neat freak" would often mention how much clutter the candles were causing. Eventually, Emma decided to work in the basement, but still go upstairs to melt her wax in the kitchen. She had more workspace and storage space down there, plus wouldn't have to disturb anyone!

FINDING THE RIGHT WORKSPACE

The good news is that you can start your candle-making business at home. Many start-up entrepreneurs, like Emma, will set up their work station in the kitchen, dining room, living room, or covered porch. Those who are fortunate enough to have a basement will have more room to work and store their supplies and candles, plus the luxury of designing their dream candle workshop.

Nevertheless, there are a few considerations you will need to make when choosing the right workspace. Here are some pointers to remember:

- Well-lighted and ventilated space.
- Clean countertop or work table.
- A space that is neither too hot nor too cold (the ideal room temperature for candle making is between 66°F and 77°F (19°C and 25°C).
- A comfortable work chair that supports good posture.
- Storage for your tools and equipment.
- Wash up station.
- Access to power.

Read about your city's zoning laws and ensure you follow the recommended procedure for operating a candle-making business at home. Since you will be working with flammable material, like hot wax, find out if you will need to obtain any permits or insurance coverage. To prevent any accidents while working with wax, here are a few housekeeping rules:

- **Never pour hot wax down your drain, as this can cause clogging.** If you would like to dispose of your wax you can either repurpose it by making a new candle or throwing it in a bucket (together with any wastewater).
- **Spread a sheet of aluminum foil or wax paper over your countertop.** This will make it easier for you to pick off any hardened wax that may have spilt on your work surface.
- **Put on an apron and gloves.** Dyes and oils can be stubborn when trying to remove them from skin or clothes. Wearing an apron and gloves can give you an extra layer of protection and prevent accidental spills. If you do get some dye on your skin, use mineral-based oils like Vaseline or Aquaphor to clean the dye from your skin.
- **When cleaning pots and oven-safe containers, line them on a baking sheet and place them upside down in the oven on low heat.** This will ensure the wax melts off and drips onto the sheet.

TOOLS AND EQUIPMENT

Making candles isn't an expensive process. You will find that many of the tools and equipment needed to make your candles can be found around the house. If not, most candle-making tools are sold for cheap at your local discount store. Here are some staples you will need:

- Rice cooker or double boiler (or preferably a wax melter if you can afford it)
- Mixing jars (plastic preferred over glass)
- Thermometer
- Kitchen scale for weighing your wax
- Apron
- Disposable gloves
- Table covers
- Candle molds
- Mixing spoons (plastic preferred over wood)
- Scissors to trim wicks
- Disposable paper towels or kitchen tea towels
- Metal scoops for hot wax
- Pliers for crimping wick sustainers
- Bucket for wax and water waste
- Candle making machine (this is optional)

Here are the specific supplies you will need to make your candles:

- Candle containers/jars
- Wax
- Wicks
- Colorants
- Fragrance
- Packaging material
- Safety labels to place on your candle containers

SAFETY PROTOCOLS WHEN MAKING YOUR CANDLES

We have already discussed a few housekeeping rules to ensure a safe workspace. However, there are other general safety rules you need to remember when making your candles. While candle-making is safe and fun, you will be working with hot wax. This means that you can injure yourself if you are not careful. Here are four safety protocols to follow to reduce the likelihood of burns and other accidents

1. Invest in Safety Equipment

It's recommended to take extra precautions when handling hot wax. Ensure that you are wearing gloves, an apron, and shoes to avoid burns. Since hot wax behaves similar to hot oil, it's better to put out a fire with a fire extinguisher, rather than water, so you can avoid any splattering of wax. Keep a first aid kit at home in case you do succumb to minor injuries.

2. Use Appropriate Candle-Making Equipment

You can make your candle-making experience safe by using the appropriate candle-making equipment. For instance, when melting wax on the stove, a double boiler will ensure your wax doesn't get too hot since the heat will be distributed evenly. A wick stabilizer is another useful tool that can keep your wicks in place while you pour hot wax inside a container or mold. This way, you won't have to hold the wick using your fingers. Lastly, make sure that wax, wicks, and other materials you use to make your candle are intended for candle-making. Read the instructions or preparation guidelines for each product you purchase and try not to deviate from them.

3. Keep Pets and Children Away

Some candle-making projects are safe for children, such as making rolled candles. However, for the most part, pets and children should be kept away from your workstation. If you do have pets at home, make sure that your house is well ventilated and windows are open when melting wax and mixing fragrances. In general, animals can be more sensitive to fragrances released during the preparation process.

4. Keep Your Workspace Clean

You can avoid accidents by keeping your workspace clean and making sure that flammable materials are stored properly. It's always good to keep a bucket near your workspace to collect waste material. Moreover, avoid leaving your wax unattended on the stove, even if you have left it on low heat.

IDENTIFY THE RIGHT SUPPLIERS

Now that you know which supplies you need, the final step will be to find the right suppliers. If you plan on starting small and testing market demand, you can purchase your supplies from a nearby hobby store or craft store online. As your business grows, and the more candles you produce, you can save costs by finding a wholesale vendor and placing bulk orders.

The right supplier will be one that can grow with you as your business grows. Ideally, you want a supplier that offers minimum and bulk quantity options, so that you can easily place larger orders when necessary. You can also look for a supplier that sells other craft materials, such as ingredients and tools to make scented soaps, so you can eventually expand your product offering without having to look for a new supplier. Lastly, since candles are brought during different holidays, festivals, and seasons, you should choose a supplier that offers a broad inventory of goods to give you plenty of options when designing your product ranges.

To seal the deal, ask suppliers you have shortlisted to provide the following documents as proof of their legitimacy:

- Business registration
- Relevant permits and licenses
- Compliance certificates
- FDA registration

You can do your own background checks too by going online and checking out their website, social media pages, and Google reviews.

Now it's your turn! Identify the perfect workspace in your home and see if it meets the requirements stated above. Next, check your kitchen, garage, and basement to see how many supplies and equipment you already have. If there are a few items you are missing, create a list and head over to your local DIY, craft, or discount store to see if you can buy them for a reasonable price.

After ensuring that everything (workspace, tools, equipment, and supplies) are in place, it's time to wear the entrepreneur hat and learn about the business side of candle-making!

PART II

BE ENLIGHTENED:

DEVELOPING AN EFFECTIVE PLAN

5

CHOOSE THE BEST BUSINESS STRUCTURE FOR YOU

In this chapter, you will learn:

- How to determine the right business structure for you by explaining each type.

CHOOSING THE RIGHT BUSINESS STRUCTURE

A business structure is the legal structure of an organization that informs how the organization is managed and the kind of legal protection it has. It determines how an organization pays its taxes, how much of the owner's assets are at risk, and any commercial benefits the organization qualifies for.

Deciding on a business structure for your candle-making business is an important decision that carries legal, operational, and financial implications. However, three factors can simplify the process of picking the right business structure for you:

1. Business Taxes

All businesses must meet federal, state, and local tax obligations. Although, the type of business structure you choose can determine which taxes you pay and how much tax you pay.

2. Industry

Some industries might recommend a certain business structure to protect owners from certain risks. In general, businesses that come with high risks often choose a structure that offers limited liability to owners.

3. Personal Liability

Some business structures, like a sole proprietorship, are easy to form and come with fewer government obligations; however, the risks are a lot higher since the owner and the business are treated as one legal entity. On the other hand, structures like corporations have added tax implications but at least owners are protected and seen as separate entities from the business. In other words, if the organization were to get in debt, the owners' assets would be safe.

Four Types of Business Structures

There are four main business structures to choose from. There isn't necessarily one that is preferred over the other since each one comes with its advantages and disadvantages. When deciding on a business structure, think about your candle-making business and what would work best for you. If you still struggle to choose a business structure, you can consult with a lawyer. Below is a breakdown of the four types of business structures:

1. Sole Proprietorship

A sole proprietorship is a business owned and run exclusively by the owner. The owner is responsible for the profits and losses of the business, as well as any liability, such as debt. Here are a few pros and cons of running a sole proprietorship

+ Pros:

- Inexpensive to form
- Relatively easy to dissolve
- No business tax obligations
- No formalities to be observed, except for bookkeeping

▬ Cons:

- Business liabilities are treated as the owner's liability
- Sole proprietorship ceases to exist upon the death of the owner

2. Partnership

A partnership is a business established and run by two or more business partners, companies, or corporations. Each partner is seen as a co-owner of the business and profits and losses are shared equally. This means that if the business incurs debt, all partners are equally liable to pay the debt. There are different types of partnerships that come with specific guidelines:

- **General partnerships:** Equal ownership of the business and all responsibilities are shared between partners (unless another arrangement is made).
- **Limited partnership:** One or more partners manage the business on a day-to-day basis and are personally liable for business debt. The rest of the partners share profits, but aren't active in the day-to-day runnings of the business and aren't personally liable for the business debt (beyond their contribution).
- **Joint venture:** A time-based partnership between two or more business owners or companies while they work together on a project. Once the project has been completed, the partnership ends.

Here are a few pros and cons of starting a partnership:

✚ **Pros:**

- You have more skills and funds to start your business
- You don't need to file paperwork with the federal government
- You don't need to pay business taxes

➖ **Cons:**

- You cannot make independent decisions
- You will need to split profits
- You aren't seen as a separate entity from your business

3. Limited Liability Company

A limited liability company sees the business owner as a separate legal entity from the business. Therefore, the owner's assets are protected should the business incur liabilities. What's more, limited liability companies can have more than one director, who are co-owners in the business. Each director also enjoys limited liability. Here are the pros and cons of starting a limiting liability company:

✚ **Pros:**

- You have the option of running it yourself or hiring a manager to run the business on your behalf
- You are protected from business liability, like debt or any legal issues

- An LLC is seen as a pass-through entity, meaning profits are shared between directors without being taxed on a company level. However, directors pay taxes on their federal income tax returns.

— **Cons:**

- For tax purposes, the government treats LLCs like partnerships, which means that the business owner is seen as benign self-employed. As such, the business owner is responsible for paying Social Security and Medicare taxes that form part of self-employment tax.
- Since LLCs don't issue stocks, it can be difficult for the business owner to raise capital to fund business operations.

4. Corporation

There are two types of corporations: a business and a non-profit corporation. Business corporations operate in the domestic or foreign business market. Similar to a limited liability company, a business corporation is a separate legal entity, meaning owners aren't held liable for business liabilities. People who own a portion of a corporation are known as shareholders, and the shareholders vote for the directors who set the policies for the corporation and hire managers to handle the day-to-day operations. Here are the pros and cons of having a corporation:

+ **Pros:**

- Shareholders have limited liability beyond their contribution
- Shareholders can transfer their ownership rights
- Selling of shares ensures the corporation has a bigger pool of capital to manage daily operations and invest in future growth

Cons:

- There are more formalities that corporations need to follow, and most decisions must be approved by the board of directors first
- Corporations may get taxed twice: once on a corporate level and again on the profits distributed to its shareholders.

Having read through each business structure, which type of business structure do you think is the best for your business objectives?

Deciding on a business structure is the first step in establishing a viable business plan. But now, we need to move on to the crux of your business—conducting in-depth market research!

6

DON'T FORGET YOUR MARKET RESEARCH

In this chapter, you will learn:

- The importance of conducting market research for your candle-making business.
- How to identify your target market, competition, and industry trends.

UNDERSTANDING YOUR MARKET

CB Insights conducted research looking into the reasons behind start-up business failures. They studied over 111 start-up businesses that had failed since 2018 and found that there were multiple reasons for business failure (CB Insights, 2019). Out of a list of 12 reasons, the second top reason for business failure was the lack of market demand. Approximately 35% of those failed businesses were solving interesting problems, not problems that addressed a market need.

What exactly is a "market need?" In general, a market need refers to a product or service that customers are looking for online or in stores. When there is a need for a product or service, the demand for it increases, meaning that customers are willing to exchange their hard-earned money for the product or service. When there is no market need, one of two things could happen: either customers are not showing interest in the product or service, or the market is already saturated with the product or service, which lowers the demand.

When you launch your candle-making business, you want customers to flock to your website and buy your candle products. But for this to happen, your candle products must fulfill a market need. Fortunately for you, since candles have a wide range of uses, you can assess the candle purchasing preferences of the market in your city and ensure that you are selling candles that are in demand throughout the year.

However, that's not the only way you can fulfill a market need. You can go the extra mile and find ways to fill a gap in the market. This is a little bit tricky to do in the candle-making industry due to how competitive the industry is, but some of the ways you can fill a gap in the market are by

- **Finding a location that isn't saturated with other candle-making businesses.** The beauty about selling online is that you can market your products to customers in different geographical locations. Through market research, you can identify cities and towns that don't have many candle businesses and ship your products to consumers in that area.
- **Incorporating new technology.** Another way to fill a gap in the market is leveraging technologies that help you make your candle-making business more competitive. For example, offering multiple payment options, flexible deliveries, and digital customizing services can make you stand out from the crowd!
- **Creating a disruptive pricing strategy.** Disruptive pricing is about creating a pricing model that the rest of the industry hasn't adopted before. By nature, it is innovative and looks at ways of responding to market needs differently. For example, subscription-based pricing models are often used in the software or printing industry. But how could this pricing model be adapted to your candle-making business?

GET TO KNOW YOUR TARGET MARKET

You don't need to worry about whether or not your candle products will sell since the candle-making industry is a profitable and prospering one! Nevertheless, the one thing you will need to spend time thinking about is the kinds of customers you will serve. Unfortunately, you can't target every type of customer because not every type of customer is interested in buying candles. You need to look for customers who are first and foremost knowledgeable about candles and secondly, see the value in purchasing them.

To find your ideal customers, you will need to identify your target market. A target market is a group of consumers that you have identified as being a good match for your products. What makes them a good match? They are educated about your products, incorporate them as part of their lifestyle, and are likely to return and purchase more products from you. If your target market is large, you can break it down into smaller market segments and use different metrics like age, location, income, or occupation to distinguish between the customers you serve. Once you have identified your target market, it becomes a lot easier to answer the following questions:

- Where can you find your customers?
- Which media channels do they use?
- What are your customers' purchasing habits?
- What kind of lifestyle do your customers live?
- How can you tailor your marketing content to attract your customers?

So, where do you begin identifying your target market? Three steps can get you started:

Step 1: Do Thorough Research

The best way to learn about your target market is to compile research about them. Of course, in the beginning, you won't know where to start, so gather statistics and go from there. The statistics will help you understand who your potential customer is and what their needs are.

Here are a few industry statistics about consumers who typically purchase candles:

- Women tend to buy candles more than men, and homeowners more than renters.
- Besides individuals, some businesses purchase candles to create an ambience, such as day spas, decor stores, yoga centers, and restaurants.
- Some candles that are produced in a specific way, like being eco-friendly or vegan, appeal to certain types of consumers.

While gathering research about your potential target market, you can also ask yourself a few questions to guide your data collection process. Here are some questions to consider:

- What is the demographic of your target market? (What is their age, gender, educational background, work status, marital status, or socio-economic status?)

- What does your target market do in their free time? (Are your potential customers hobbyists? Do they enjoy getting massages? Or do they enjoy hosting friends and family at home?)
- Where does your target market live? (Is your target market-based in the same city, town, or country, or do they come from different parts of the world?)
- How often does your target market purchase candles from your business? (Are there specific days, seasons, or festivals that your potential customers support your business?)

Step 2: Segment Your Market

At this stage, you should have a lot of information about your target market. However, to better understand your target market and make it easier to address their needs, you must segment your market into groups of buyers. For instance, you can have 100 people who purchase candles, but out of that number, 70 are women and 30 are men, or 60% purchase scented candles while 40% purchase unscented candles. You can segment your market using different factors like age, gender, candle preferences, and so on. Looking at your different market segments, you might decide to focus on one or two segments as you launch your business and slowly add new segments the bigger your business grows.

Step 3: Define Your Ideal Customers

Based on the segments you have decided to market your products to, you can define your ideal customers. Here are a few questions that can help you create a rich and detailed profile of your ideal customers:

- Is your ideal customer male or female?
- How old are they?
- What do they do for a living?
- Are they single or married?
- Do they have children? If so, how old are their children?
- What is their average income?
- What motivates your ideal customer to buy candles from your business?
- What other similar products do they buy from other businesses?
- Which social media platforms do they use? And how often are they online?

At this point, you have found your target market, divided it into various market segments, and chosen one or a few segments to focus on. Moreover, you have created a comprehensive profile of your ideal customer, which will make it easy for you to customize your marketing material to suit their preferences.

KNOW YOUR COMPETITION

As mentioned earlier, start-ups don't perform well when they can't address a market need or fill a market gap. The candle-making market has tough competition since there are only so many variations one can make to a candle. This means that you should aim to produce candles that are better in quality, pricing, or packaging than your competitors.

In order to determine the right approach and strategy for your candle-making business, you must extensively study your competitors. Remember that you will be competing with local candle-makers, as well as those who are selling their products online. When studying your local and online competitors, analyze how they sell their products, who their customers are, and at what price point do their candles go for. Here are a few questions that can guide you as you research your competitors:

- Which other top small businesses are you up against (locally and online)?
- Which other well-established businesses are you up against (locally and online)?
- What type of candles do your competitors make?
- Are they homemade or factory-made?
- What are the top five common candle scents your competitors use, across the board?
- What type of packaging do your competitors use?
- How does your local community or online community perceive your competitors? What are some of the reviews your competitors have received?
- How do your competitors advertise their candles? Do they offer promotions or discounts? Are there other incentives they advertise, like free shipping?

When Emma started her candle-making business, she ran out of mason jars and decided to pour her candle into everyday drinking glasses. Some candles were in martini glasses, others in champagne glasses, and other unique glasses she could find around the house. When she listed her products, she was nervous that her customers—upmarket homeowners who enjoyed hosting guests—would find these candle containers to be rather strange or inappropriate. To her surprise, her customers absolutely loved the candles, so much so that her stock was sold out within the first week! By making a mistake, Emma had identified another way to serve her customers' needs, and the best part was that she was the only business in her area that had created such a novel product.

Sometimes, you learn how to outperform your competitors by simply doing trial and error. Find new ways of combining colors, scents, or creating innovative candle containers. You never know when you will accidentally create a product that your customers didn't even know they needed!

If the thought of conducting market research on your own sounds daunting, there are alternative ways to receive the much-needed help and support that you need. In the next chapter, we will discuss available resources that can offer you tips, tutorials, and industry best practices for your candle-making business.

7

GET SOME HELP AND LEARN MORE ABOUT THE CANDLE MAKING WORLD

In this chapter, you will learn:

- The best websites and forums to know more about candle-making and best practices.

SUPPORT IS CLOSER THAN YOU THINK

On her second week into building her candle-making business, Emma seemed to have hit a brick wall. When she was testing a batch of her candles, all of them melted unevenly. The candles melted through the center creating a tunnel and leaving a lot of solid wax on the sides. As a first-time candle-maker, Emma had no idea how to fix this problem.

While researching for potential solutions online, she came across Facebook groups for candle makers. Some groups shared information about the best places to buy supplies, other groups shared tutorial videos, and one of them, in particular, offered support to first-time candle-makers. She joined the groups, introduced herself and her business, and connected with so many kindred spirits, from different parts of the country, who shared the same passion she had for candle-making. Emma was able to ask questions, get expert advice, and find the best way to avoid tunneling. Later on, as she developed more experience, she was able to share some hacks that could help other candle-makers produce the best quality candles too!

BEST FREE WEBSITES AND BLOGS ABOUT CANDLE-MAKING

There are thousands of resources about candle-making available online. However, to narrow your search, here are some of the best websites that offer expert advice and information about candle-making:

1. National Candle Association

The sole trade association representing candle suppliers and manufacturers based in the United States.

2. CandleScience

America's leading candle supplier, offering a variety of products, from an assortment of candle wax to a wide range of fragrance oils.

3. CraftServer

A public forum where candle-makers meet to discuss techniques, share advice, and ask questions about the candle-making process.

4. Candle Cauldron

A website offering tips and resources about the candle-making process. Whether you are new to the candle-making business or a seasoned veteran, you will find a community of candle-makers who will share ideas and tips with you, or if you are looking for a marketplace, you can sell or swap candles, candle supplies, or equipment with other candle-makers.

5. Candle Gossip

If you are looking for the latest craft ideas or hottest trends in the candle market, you can visit the Candle Gossip. You will find inspiration for scents, colors, or candle containers for your next candle range, plus specific trends for various seasons or festivals in the year.

6. Armatage Candle Company Blog

This website hosts a collection of free articles on candle-making. On there, you can find articles about legal considerations for making candles, different types of wicks and which ones work for different types of candles, and how to create your first line of candles. There are also candle-making online courses that you can take which teach you various methods of making candles at home.

7. Candle Junkies

A community blog run by candle lovers who review different types of candles in the market. By going through their collection of articles, you will find opinion pieces about which fragrances work best on candles, reviews on the latest candle trends, and which brands are leading in the market.

Besides going on websites and blogs, you can also browse through social media platforms, such as Facebook, to find groups for candle-makers like yourself. Here are a few Facebook groups to consider:

1. DIY Candle Making Beginner to Advanced (112,000+ members)

The group offers support to new candle-makers, particularly those with candle-making business, and shares videos, how-to guides, and general information on how to get started.

2. Candle Makers Club (21,000+ members)

The group encourages discussions around candle-making and the various steps involved in the process, such as how to choose the right wax or wick for your candle, or general reviews on the best candle-making supplies in the market.

3. Candle Making by Candle Makers (40,000+ members)

A community of candle-makers who share a love for candle-making and offer support to one another. In this group, you can ask questions, raise concerns about your candle-making process, and share photos of your beautiful work of art.

4. Candle Makers Resource Group (65,000+ members)

A community of candle-makers who share their successes and failures during the process of making candles. Members are encouraged to ask questions, share tips, and post pictures and videos of their crafted candles.

5. Makers Circle Candle Making (34,000+ members)

A candle-making forum managed by the Wooden Wick Co. Members are encouraged to have discussions about the candle-making process and learn from one another. Some of the topics discussed on the forum include fragrances, waxes, and different types of candles.

Have you tried joining one of the Facebook groups listed above? If not, why not give it a shot!

With all the information you have gathered so far from researching your candle-making business, the next step is to compile your data into one document and create your business blueprint—also known as your business plan.

8

CREATE YOUR CANDLE-MAKING BUSINESS PLAN

In this chapter you will learn:

- The general structure of a business plan to help you draft your own plan for your candle-making business.

WHY CREATING A BUSINESS PLAN IS IMPORTANT

There is a famous quote by Benjamin Franklin that says, "If you fail to plan, you are planning to fail" (Goodreads, 2019). Many entrepreneurs overlook the process of drafting a business plan, although creating one will prove invaluable for the sustainability of your business. Think of a business plan as being the roadmap that shows you how to run your business and which opportunities to leverage. When compiled correctly, your business plan can help you define your strategy, identify challenges to business growth, and understand what resources you will need to legalize your business and begin your operations.

Moreover, your business plan can help you with the general day-to-day business tasks, such as budgeting, estimates for turnover, managing your team of employees, workplace health and safety, and so on.

How to Structure Your Business Plan

Most entrepreneurs treat business plans as just another plain and boring company document. They don't invest nearly as much time and research into compiling this blueprint as they should. Oftentimes, the consequence of not doing careful planning is that these businesses lack a clear focus and direction. Soon, they become like any other business competing in their respective market, rather than offering a unique value proposition and running their enterprise differently.

Creating your business plan allows you to think of ways to stand out from the rest and create a unique path that you will follow. It is your personal blueprint that highlights your strengths and weaknesses, as well as identified gaps in the market you can capitalize on.

Even though your business plan won't look the same as any other business owners', there are a few general components that you must include when researching and compiling your business plan:

1. Executive Summary

A concise overview of your business strategy and operations, as well as the keys to business growth (or any other unique value you bring to the market or opportunity you have identified).

2. Business Overview

A brief overview of your company vision, mission statement, and objectives. Here, you can also discuss your company name, logo, culture, and brand, and explain why you have chosen these particular elements.

3. Products and Services

A section that goes into detail about the products and services you will offer as you launch your business. You can explain the components of your products, how you will produce your products, any variations to your products, and so forth.

4. Market Analysis

Your market research, including industry analysis, trend analysis, competitor analysis, and target market analysis, will fall under this section of your business plan. Ideally, you will need to identify a market need that your business can respond to, or a gap in the market that other businesses haven't taken advantage of.

5. Sales and Marketing

Share details about your pricing strategy, promotional strategies, and the various sales channels you will use to sell your products. You can also discuss your product's unique selling point (USP), which are the factors that distinguish your products from your competitor's products.

6. Management Team

An overview of your organizational hierarchy, management team, and job descriptions of each employee in your business.

7. Operations Plan

Your operations plan includes a breakdown of your business processes, systems, software, e-commerce website, logistics plan, and any other factor involved in the day-to-day running of your business. You can include the step-by-step process of making your candles, the process and safety protocol for operating certain equipment, and details about storage, warehousing, shipping, and deliveries of your products to customers.

8. Financial Plan

This is usually the final section in your business plan that includes spreadsheets calculating your start-up costs, profit and loss estimates, cash flow statements, break-even analysis, and balance sheet. If you are planning on seeking financing, this section will help lenders assess the profitability and risk associated with your business.

After you have compiled your business plan, refer to this checklist below to see whether you have included all of the necessary information:

- Have you explained the purpose, mission, and objectives of your business?

- Have you set metric-based goals for areas of growth in your business?
- Have you created robust strategies to reduce as much risk as possible during the first few years of running your business?
- Have you found ways to differentiate your business from other businesses in your industry?
- Do you have a solid understanding of your customer, how to reach them, and what to sell them?

Now that you have learned about the components of a business plan, make a rough draft of your candle-making business plan by following the elements listed above.

The last section of a business plan is always related to the business's financial projections. To help you with your calculations, the next chapter will discuss the financial aspect of a candle-making business.

PART III

KNOW YOUR SCENTS AND DOLLARS:

CRUNCHING THE NUMBERS IN CANDLE-MAKING

9

DETERMINE YOUR EXPENSES

In this chapter, you will learn:

- The breaks down of the costs that a candle-making business usually entails, which are also related to the early chapters.

CANDLE-MAKING BUSINESS START-UP COSTS

One of the major incentives for starting a candle-making business is how little start-up capital you need. Now, you might be wondering: *How little is little?* The truth is it depends on the size of your business and how many supplies and administrative costs you need to pay for. Generally speaking though, you could start your candle-making business with as little as $500. This usually works when you already have most of the supplies you will need to make your candles and already have somewhat of a customer base so you don't need to invest in creating new marketing channels. However, if you are starting from scratch and need to buy supplies and create new systems and processes in your business, your start-up costs can reach upwards of $1,000.

Creating a Start-up Budget

Your start-up costs include the once-off expenses you will need to pay to get your business off the ground. For example, when you start a business, you need to register it as a legal entity, purchase supplies to produce your products, and create a website so your customers can discover you online. All of these tasks require money, although, for the most part, you only pay once or annually (renewing your business licenses is one expense you will need to pay on an annual basis).

Here are a few examples of different kinds of start-up costs:

1. Supplies

These expenses include materials or ingredients required to make your products. Some of the standard supplies you will need for candle-making are wax, wicks, fragrance, and colorants. You will also need to purchase candle-making tools, like candle molds and melting pots; however, once you have bought these, you won't have to buy them again (unless when you are upgrading your tools).

2. Administration

These expenses are associated with running your business activities, such as paying for the ink in your printer, taxes (business, personal, and property taxes), insurance cover, social media advertising, or research and development expenses. If you are going to take out a business loan, interest payable on your loan would also fall under this category.

3. Facilities

Costs that are associated with the physical location where you will do business are known as facilities expenses. Regardless of whether you run your business from a leased studio or in your basement, you may want to consider the cost of water, electricity, or telephone bill, which are related to running your business. If your cash flow statement is healthy, you may also want to consider having your business pay rent for operating at your home.

4. Labor

When you start your candle-making business, you may be the only employee managing your operations. You can choose to pay yourself a salary, as a full-time or contract worker. Other expenses that fall under this category include firms whose services you outsource, like the accounting firm that helps you compile your books or the marketing firm that handles your social media pages.

Here is an example of what your start-up budget would look like as a spreadsheet:

Item	Budgeted Amount	Actual Amount	Variance	% Variance
Start-up Costs				
Starting inventory	$150	$187.93	($37.93)	(24.93%)
Licenses and permits	$125	$125	$0.00	0%
Cash	$1,000	$750	$250	25%
Subtotal	**$1,275**	**$1,062.93**	**$212.07**	**16.63%**
Supply Costs				
Molds	$60	$72.25	($12.25)	(20.42%)
Wax	$150	$152.75	($2.75)	(1.83%)
Wicks	$14.50	$14.50	$0.00	0%
Subtotal	**$224.50**	**$229.50**	**($5.00)**	**(2.23%)**

Administrative Expenses				
Insurance	$300	$292.14	$7.86	2.92%
Office Supplies	$50	$25.76	$24.24	48.48%
Income taxes	$500	$514.66	($14.66)	(2.93%)
Social media	$125	$125	$0	0%
Website development	$400	$400	$0	0%
Printing	$30	$22.25	$7.75	25.83%
Subtotal	**$1,405**	**$1,379.81**	**$25.19**	**1.79%**
Facilities Expense				
Telephone	$55	$55	$0	0%
Subtotal	**$55**	**$55**	**$0**	**0%**
Labor Expenses				
Full-time labor (self)	$3,500	$3,500	$0	0%
Professional fees	$1,500	$1,500	$0	0%
Subtotal	**$5,000**	**$5,000**	**$0**	**0%**

How to Reduce Start-up Expenses

Starting a business can be expensive if you don't have a strategy to reduce your start-up costs. Even though some expenses are set in stone (such as the fee for registering your business), you can find ways of cutting down the budget for other expenses. Here are five ways that you can significantly reduce your start-up costs:

1. Make a Priority List

For this strategy, you will need to refer to your business plan. Take a look at your operations section in your business plan and identify expenses that are non-negotiable for the first 6 months of your business. These could include equipment, packaging material, and candle-making supplies. Total this list and compare it with your original start-up expense budget. The aim is to only focus on essential expenses and as time goes on, include other operational expenses that can make running your candle-making business a lot smoother.

2. Track Your Spending

Keep a record of everything you purchase from the very beginning of running your business. Any business-related expense, including insurance, advertising, and a consultation with a graphic designer should be tracked on a spreadsheet. Getting into the habit of tracking your expenses can help you regulate how you spend your money and do away with frivolous expenses.

3. Hire With Intention

Labor costs can be expensive, especially for a start-up business that isn't achieving consistent sales yet. Think about what role you need an employee to serve in your business and whether the value they will add is worth the amount of money you are paying them. It's better to hire contractors for a specific time it takes to get a task done than hire a full-time employee. If you can, try to automate as many small, repetitive tasks that can be done by software or online tool so you can free up a lot of your time and focus on more labor-intensive tasks, like producing candles.

No matter which tactics you use to reduce costs, careful planning and prioritizing your expenses is the best way to manage your start-up costs. Create a budget for your first two months in business. Estimate the cost of supplies and overheads, administration, facilities, marketing, and labor. Remember to focus on the essentials and don't forget to pay yourself an hourly wage for your time and effort as a business owner, too!

Now that you know how much a candle-making business costs, you can follow through with sourcing funds if you don't have enough capital.

10

FUND YOUR BUSINESS

In this chapter, you will learn:

- How to source funds, especially if you do not have enough capital to kick-start your candle-making business.

TIPS FOR SECURING START-UP FUNDING

When Emma decided to start her candle-making business, she realized she didn't have sufficient savings in her bank account to last her through the first year. Even though she knew it takes money to make money, she didn't allow the lack of funds to get her down. Instead, she invested a lot of time in creating her business plan so that she could appeal to as many investors or lenders as possible.

Here are a few tips that helped Emma secure funding for her business:

1. Scrutinize Your Business Model

Emma knew that investors don't buy into ideas, they buy into the future revenue of a business. In other words, an investor wants to know that in a few years, they will be able to gain considerable returns on their investment. Thus, they are interested in proven and viable business models. Emma took it upon herself to scrutinize her business model to ensure it could bring as much profit as she predicted. Having a clear path to profits made it easy for investors to assess future returns of her candle-making business.

2. Focus on Improving Your Business

It wasn't easy for Emma to secure an investor. She went to several meetings and was turned down countless times by people who didn't believe in her product. Instead of giving up, Emma focused on improving her business processes, learning more about the candle-making industry, and staying updated with trends. Each time she learned something new, she tweaked her business plan, refined her products, and optimized her online sales. All of the time and effort she was investing in making her business better, caused investors to stop and notice her.

3. Keep a Track Record of Your Business Performance

During the first year of running her candle-making business, Emma's sales fluctuated from month to month. On some months, she would earn upwards of $1,000 and on other months just below $1,000. Instead of hiding her numbers, she recorded every transaction, even when she was making a loss. When investors had a look at her financial statements, they were able to see the true potential of her candle-making business. Yes, there were bad months, but her records showed great potential for success and proved that she was operating a legitimate business.

4. Ask for Support

After Emma had maxed out her savings and could no longer tap into her line of credit at the bank, she reached out to close friends and family and asked if anyone was willing to loan her money with interest. Two close friends agreed to loan Emma money and told her she could pay them back within 12 months —no interest charged!

5. Learn to Adapt to Your Business Needs

Instead of waiting for an investor to agree to fund her business, Emma took the proactive approach and looked for ways she could reduce expenses so that she had more cash reserves each month. She managed to save costs on supplies by finding a more affordable supplier, and this gave her an extra $200 in cash each month. She reinvested the extra cash into her business and was able to increase her marketing budget (a decision that brought in 35% more revenue in sales).

How to Create a Funding Proposal

A funding proposal is a document that summarizes what your business is about, how much funding you need, and what is in it for potential investors. Unlike your business plan, your funding proposal doesn't need to be extensive; however, you will need to add as much statistical and factual information about your industry and business as you can.

Potential investors are looking for a few things in your funding proposal: Hard facts, honesty, and realistic projections. It's not advised to exaggerate your figures as a way to impress your potential investors. The more realistic your numbers look, the more comfortable investors will be funding your business. Keep in mind that if your funding proposal is rejected or unsuccessful, there are other ways of raising capital, which are discussed in the section below.

With that said, here are a few tips for creating your funding proposal:

1. Include an Executive Summary

Similar to your business plan, your funding proposal will need to begin with an executive summary or proposal overview. This must be written in a way that captures the investor's interest and makes them excited to read further. Keep your executive summary about a page in length and only include the main points, such as your business overview, target market, your unique selling point, and any gaps in the market you have identified. You can also briefly mention why you are seeking funding and how much money you are hoping to raise.

2. Put Your Offer on the Table

The funding proposal must include a section where you explain what you are willing to offer potential investors. Your offer must be valuable enough that investors are willing to part with their hard-earned money. Some investors may prefer equity (shares in your business), while others are happy to loan you money if they can charge you a certain amount of interest. Another way to make your offer more attractive is to explain the benefits and desirability of your product and why it is better than your competitors. For instance, are you perhaps producing a new candle that hasn't been seen in the market?

3. Be Honest About Your Numbers

Of course, the funding proposal wouldn't be complete without a detailed look into the numbers. If you are approaching a seasoned investor, they will be able to look at your projections and quickly pick up on any discrepancies. Therefore, be honest when estimating your figures and add as much detail as you can. Since you are starting a new business, you won't have any historical financial data to justify your figures. In this case, you can base your numbers on current industry data, the size of your target market, current candle sales in your area, or online, and other relevant statistics.

A comprehensive proposal stating who you are, what you are willing to offer in exchange for capital, and how the funds will help you grow the business and deliver returns for your investor is what you will need to present when seeking funding. While waiting on the verdict on your proposal, you can try the following tactics to raise capital for your business.

The Various Ways to Raise Capital

Very soon, you will be in Emma's position and look for ways to save costs and increase your revenue each month. Of course, finding an investor who believes in your candle-making business enough would be ideal, however, if that's not possible, you will need to look for other ways of raising capital.

Here are some of the legitimate options you have for funding your business:

- **Traditional bank loans:** A common way to secure funding for your business involves getting approved for a loan through a bank. To improve your chances of being approved, you will need to have a comprehensive business plan and solid credit history.

- **SBA loans:** The U.S. Small Business Administration can serve as a guarantor and help you get approved for SBA-backed microloans.
- **Venture capital:** Venture capitalists are investors who specialize in offering loans to businesses in exchange for equity (a portion of ownership) in the business. Not only do venture capitalists offer access to capital, but they can also share their skills, knowledge, and network so your business receives the support it needs.
- **Crowdfunding:** A new way for entrepreneurs to secure funding is through crowdfunding websites, like kickstarter. You can create a goal and raise capital from a large community of people. The upside is that the funds you receive are treated as a donation, meaning you don't need to repay those who supported your crowdfunding drive with cash or equity.
- **Business credit card:** A revolving line of credit, like a business credit card, can help you settle minor business expenses while building your business's credit profile, which eventually can give you more access to credit.

Having looked through each source of funding, which ones are you compelled to try?

The money talk is not over yet. Once you have accounted for all your expenses and know how much it costs to produce each candle, you will need to set your selling price. The following chapter will show you how to do this!

MAKE SURE THE PRICE IS RIGHT

In this chapter you will learn:

- Different pricing strategies and find the best one for your candle-making business.
- How to properly price your candles to ensure maximum profits.

GETTING THE PRICING RIGHT

When Emma grew confident in her ability to make homemade crafted candles, she decided it was time to expand her reach by selling at craft fairs and trade events. However, her first attempt was not as successful as she had hoped. She found herself selling alongside candle artisans who were selling their candles at basically the same price point as she was. She realized that while she had quality candles, the premium price was driving away consumers who would rather have same-priced products but were made by known artists, or those who would go for lesser-quality products but less expensive at the same time. She realized that she needed to go back to the drawing board and evaluate her pricing strategy again to make sure she could compete with other businesses.

Pricing Strategies to Consider When Setting Your Price

A major question that all candle-making business owners will have is: *How much can I make from my candles?* After all, as passionate as you are about making candles, you want to ensure your business remains profitable.

The general price range for candles in the industry is between $5 and $30, sometimes even more depending on the quality of the candle (such as the value of the scent or the container it is placed in), and the specific target market a business is selling to.

You might be tempted to price your candles toward the lower end of the price range, although this strategy doesn't always work. When your candles are priced too low, customers may assume they are cheap mass-market candles. However, making your candles too expensive might send customers running away, especially if the quality isn't the same as other upmarket candle brands.

Here are a few different ways you can set your prices for your candles. Note that once you choose your preferred strategy, you need to commit to it throughout your product range:

- **Penetration pricing:** Analyze your competitor's pricing and set a much lower price than them. While this strategy will help you make initial sales when you launch your business, it isn't sustainable in the long run.

- **Skimming pricing:** Set a high price for your newest products, then as the novelty wears off, reduce the price and prepare to launch a new product range at the highest price. While this strategy allows you to maximize profits on new product releases, some customers may become frustrated that they bought your product at a higher price than other customers.
- **Premium pricing:** Set your prices at the highest range in the market to create perceived value. The upside of using this strategy is that your profit margins will be higher than your competitors since you will be charging more for your products; however, it can backfire if customers don't perceive your product as being of high value.
- **Psychological pricing:** Slightly alter your prices to make it seem like your customers are getting more for their money. For example, pricing your candles at $19.99 instead of $20, or offering a "buy one get one free" promotion makes a customer think they are getting a better deal for their money.
- **Bundle pricing:** Sell two or more products together, at one price. This strategy can help you add more value to your customers' purchases, while also introducing new samples or products. However, products bought in bundles will likely sell less when bought as individual items, since customers save more money buying them in a set or bundle.

- **Competitive pricing:** Set your product at the same price point as the current market rate. Instead of selling higher or lower than competitors, you would price your products within the same range. This strategy can help you stay competitive, especially when you are operating in a saturated industry.
- **Cost-plus pricing:** Take the amount of money it costs you to produce your product and add a percentage mark-up (profit margin) to determine your selling price. While this strategy can help you predict your sales, it can also cause you to miss out on opportunities to lower your price and increase sales through promotions.

Play around with the different pricing strategies and see which ones would be suitable for your candles.

Now that you've done your math, it's time to move on to the legal aspect of your candle-making business.

PART IV

KINDLE THE CANDLES:

MAKING YOUR BUSINESS LEGIT

12

CHOOSE YOUR BUSINESS NAME

In this chapter, you will learn:

- How to pick the ideal name for your business so you can hit the ground running.

FACTORS TO CONSIDER WHEN CHOOSING A BUSINESS NAME

According to Small Biz Genius, 72% of the most recognizable brand names are made-up words or acronyms (Vojinovic, 2022). Take the world's largest search engine, Google, for example. The brand name Google came about due to a misspelling of a real word –*googol*– which is a math term used to signify a large number. The name googol was supposed to represent the vast amount of information one could find on the search engine.

An effective way to make your candle-making business stand out from the rest is to have a unique business name. You can't underestimate the significance of a name, since it is perhaps the first way a potential customer gets to know about your business. When your business name appears on search engines, social media feeds, or on your existing customer's lips, its appeal can make people curious about what you are about.

Google might have worked for a search engine, but what kind of name works for a candle-making business? The best names for candle-making businesses are short and simple. This makes them memorable, easy to look up on the internet and work well on many logos and brand designs. Come up with a list of names and search to see if there is a domain name available for your website before committing to a business name.

This is important because you want your business name to be consistent throughout your marketing platforms. Therefore, if your business name is "Wick-ed", then your domain name should be "wick-ed.com" and your social media accounts should all be "Wick-ed" or "Wick-ed Canada" if you want to make it clear that you only operate within a specific region. While it's not mandatory to register a trademark, you can choose to do so. Once again, first, run a trademark search before committing to your business name so that if you decide to trademark your name in future you won't have any issues.

Here are a few more tips that can help you when thinking about a name for your business

- Short and catchy names are easier to remember than long names most people cannot pronounce.
- Do a quick internet and social media search and make sure there is no other candle-making business that has the same name as yours.
- Your business name should be relevant and appropriate to your product and service offerings.
- Including relevant keywords like "wax" or "candle" in your name can boost your SEO ranking.
- Go for a name that can easily accommodate new products and services in the future, rather than a name that is specific to one type of product or service.

After finding the perfect name for your business, it's time to make it official! The next chapter will tell you about all the things you need to secure before you can legally open your business.

13

REGISTRATION, PERMITS, AND INSURANCE

In this chapter you will learn:

- How to make your candle-making business more legitimate by registering your business, securing the necessary permits, and getting insurance.

REGISTERING YOUR BUSINESS

While registering your business may not be the most fun aspect of the candle-making business, doing the necessary paperwork is an absolutely crucial step and it's better to do it now than later. In order to pay your taxes, approach financial lenders, or open a bank account, you will need to have the legal paperwork for your business.

For any other business, the state you decide to register your business in, won't really matter. However, since not every state has candle suppliers, it would be advantageous to base your business in a state where you have access to multiple candle supply stores. If you are willing to relocate, this could be a great opportunity for your business.

In general, the process of registering your business requires you to select a company structure (refer to Chapter 5), but most states also require that you register your business name at the same time as registering your business. Each state may have its own process for registering a business name, so check with your local authorities to find out how to get the process started.

Besides registering your business entity and name, there are a few other applications you will need to complete, such as:

1. Federal Employer Identification Number (FEIN)

The FEIN is a tax number that registers your business with the Internal Revenue Service (IRS). Even if you don't currently have employees, you will still be required to have a FEIN, except if you have registered your business as a sole proprietorship or single-owner LLC. In this case, you can use your own social security number while you don't have any employees.

2. Sales Tax Permit

Since your objective is to sell candle products, you will need to obtain a sales tax permit, or business tax number. The permit registers your candle-making business with the Department of Revenue, or any other equivalent state tax agency. As soon as you hire employees, you will most likely need to have a sales tax permit.

3. Resale Certificate

If you plan on selling candle-making supplies, like candle fragrances and wax, you can buy these supplies tax-free if you have a resale certificate (also known as a seller's permit). When you buy inventory, instead of paying the sales tax to your supplier, you can charge the sales tax to your customer. Nevertheless, for regular business supplies (stock that isn't being resold), you will still need to pay the sales tax on goods.

4. Certificate of Occupancy

Whether you are looking to operate your candle-making business in a commercial space, like an office building, or at home, you will need to obtain a certificate of occupancy. You can apply for the certificate of occupancy from your city or county office. You will need to ensure that your office space or workspace at home complies with local zoning regulations and building codes so that it can operate legally in your chosen location.

Running a candle-making business also requires you to obtain several licenses and permits from your local, state, and federal government. There is a range of licenses and permits, each serving a different purpose. For instance, some ensure that you are operating your business legally and others ensure you are complying with health and safety codes. When it comes to health and safety licenses, you may need to obtain licenses at the local, city, and state levels. They may also be specific licenses that your particular state requires. Go onto your state government's website and inquire about the licenses needed to operate a candle-making business.

Lastly, you will also need to consider getting insurance for your business, especially if you intend on hiring employees. For example, you might want to consider taking out worker's compensation or unemployment insurance for your employees. If your employees will be working with flammable materials, taking out additional disability insurance may protect you and your employees in the event of accidental physical injuries. Other types of insurance you might consider taking out include:

- **General liability:** This type of insurance covers a variety of liabilities your business may be exposed to, including injuries at work and property damage. Oftentimes, business owners get this comprehensive insurance cover instead of paying for different types of insurance.

- **Business property:** Insurance that covers your business assets, including your physical building, supplies, and equipment.
- **Commercial auto:** This type of insurance covers your business vehicles. This kind of insurance is useful if you intend on operating an online delivery service in your local area and rely on your company-owned vehicles to move products from your business location to your customers' locations.
- **Professional liability:** Insurance that protects you when a customer claims that your products caused them to suffer a loss due to an error in your product.

Not every insurer offers cover for every type of business liability. Do your due diligence and compare different insurance products before settling for one that offers your business the most protection.

After surviving the challenging legal part of your business, it's time for the fun part—getting your product out to the market!

PART V

MAKE IT "LIT":

CREATING YOUR OWN BRAND

14

MARKET YOUR PRODUCT

In this chapter you will learn:

- How to properly promote your candles to the market, covering both the traditional and modern marketing techniques.

DETERMINE YOUR UNIQUE SELLING POINT (USP)

Jonathan Lister, the VP of Global Sales Solutions at LinkedIn, said "Speak to your audience in their language about what's in their heart" (Ganassini, 2016). By this, he meant that the best way to market a product or service isn't about selling its specific features or the benefits it comes with, but instead to show a customer how your product or service can improve their everyday life.

If you think about the utility of a candle, it is to bring light into a space. But nowadays, there are so many products in the market that bring light into an area. In fact, some products are even better at adding or enhancing light in an area than candles. Therefore, marketing your candles' utility won't pull at your customer's heartstrings.

You need to think deeper and find the unspoken appeal that a candle has with customers. Besides adding light, what other reasons would cause a customer to pay upward of $30 for a candle, monthly? You may find that for some customers, candles bring a sense of calm and relaxation to a room, while others cannot celebrate occasions without having candles as a decorative element. In your bid to reel in customers to buy your candles, leverage on the unspoken appeal that the product can give them.

This unspoken appeal is usually called a unique selling point (USP). It refers to the characteristics of a product that distinguish it from other products competing in the market. Imagine that your candles were among many on a store shelf. A shopper walked through the aisle and was inundated with so many buying options. Even though the shelf had a lot of the same product, each candle—including yours—looked different from the rest. Now, think about what would make the shopper pick your candle out of the rest. Whatever list of factors you can name will be your unique selling point.

Tips for Creating a Unique Selling Point

Your USP shouldn't merely stand out in your product or packaging, it should also be evident on your website, social media pages, as well as your customer service management. Every time your target market encounters your business, there should be specific elements to your marketing and communication that leaves a positive impression.

Below are a few tips when creating a USP for your candle-making business:

1. Step Inside Your Ideal Customer's Shoes

To understand what matters most to your ideal customer, you need to think about several aspects of their life, like what gives them a sense of purpose, what kind of goals they are working toward, and what kind of lifestyle they aspire to live. Here are a few questions to think about

- What does your ideal customer *really* want in life?
- How can your candles solve their problems?
- What would motivate your ideal customer to purchase your candles?
- How would your candles help your ideal customer success in life?

2. Be Clear About the Solution You Bring

Remember that consumers are confronted with hundreds of businesses daily. What can make your business stand out from the rest is being clear about the specific problem you have identified and the solution you offer to customers. For example, a cosmetic company sells confidence, glamor, and beauty, on top of selling their cosmetic products. Confidence, glamor, and beauty are the unspoken appeal that cosmetic products have to customers. Thus, in their marketing and promotional material, cosmetic companies show faces of beautiful and confident men and women and add copies like "glow" and "happiness," to clearly communicate their solution.

Similarly, your USP should sell the solution your candles can bring to your customers' lives. Besides its decorative purpose, what other problems do your candles solve?

3. Create an Elevator Pitch

Now that you have stepped in your ideal customer's shoes and thought about the solutions you bring to the table, create a 30-60 second elevator pitch explaining your USP—using your customer's language (in words and terms they would understand). This exercise will help to simplify your USP and make it easier to translate it on various marketing and communication platforms. Here is a simple template to help you prepare your pitch:

For [describe ideal customer], [your business name] is [1st unique selling point] that provides [2nd unique selling point]. Unlike [name one or two competitors], [your business name] is the only company that [3rd unique selling point].

As you can see in the template above, there are three opportunities for you to list the unique characteristics of your product that set it apart from your competitors. Your selling points can be based on any of the following factors:

- Regional or exclusive scents
- Unusual candle designs
- Impact on the environment
- Specific uses (i.e. Aromatherapy candles)
- Unique buying options (i.e. Shopping online, delivered straight to your door)
- Added services that come with purchasing your products

WORK ON YOUR BRAND ELEMENTS

A brand is a persona you create that resembles everything your ideal customer stands for and aspires to in life. Most times, your customers won't interact with your business directly, unless they are speaking to a customer service agent. Instead, they will interact with your brand, which is the human aspect of your business.

There are many elements to branding, the main ones being your brand logo, colors and fonts, and label designs. Let's look at each element and how you can achieve a cohesive and aesthetically pleasing brand across your product range and marketing platforms.

1. Logo Design

The complexity or simplicity of your logo is dependent on your brand's style, culture, and look and feel. For example, if you have an eco-friendly brand, then your logo may be minimalistic with clean lines and a slick font. What matters most when designing your logo is whether it can work well with your packaging and candle labels. You may also want to create a logo that incorporates your brand's color palette and typography so that the logo that appears on your products is the same one that appears on your website and social media pages.

2. Brand Fonts and Color Palette

When it comes to creating a brand that customers easily recognize in stores or online, consistency is key. You have hundreds of different color shades and fonts to choose from, but not every color or font will reinforce what your brand is about. Consider using two or three typefaces across your label design, packaging, website, and social media platforms. It is recommended to use a Serif font as your default "Heading 1" text and a Sans Serif font for your default "Heading 2" text. Heading 1 text is normally used when writing out your product names or page titles and Heading 2 for any announcements, subtitles, or highlighting product features.

When selecting your color palette, stick to a range of 3-5 main colors. You may decide to use some colors more than other colors and create primary and secondary brand colors. Instead of playing around with different color shades, you can use monochromatic colors, such as black and white, and add one extra pop of color. The goal when choosing your palette is to find the best way to make your brand stand out, while also being true to who you are.

3. Candle Labels

Selecting your logo, fonts, and colors will make your job designing candle labels a lot easier. Besides the aesthetics of your label, there are a few elements that must be included on each candle label

- Your label must make it clear that the product is a candle.
- It must include your company logo, name, and contact details.
- If you are producing a scented candle, the label must include the description of the fragrance used.
- You must indicate what type of wax or waxes were used to produce your candle.
- Your label should also include the weight of your candle in both grams and ounces (this should be the weight of the candle alone, without the container).
- Since a candle is flammable, your label must include warnings and safety instructions, such as "Keep out of reach of pets and children," or "Keep away from flammable objects."

MARKETING TOOLS AND METHODS

Once your brand elements are ready, you can prepare to market your candle-making business! Remember, your marketing content must match your brand colors, fonts, and designs, so that you can quickly become a recognizable brand across your marketing platform.

The oldest and most effective type of marketing is word-of-mouth advertising, but you cannot rely on it alone to attract customers. You will need to create a comprehensive marketing plan that includes both online and offline marketing tools and methods. Let's discuss a few online and offline marketing tools that can give your business a good amount of exposure:

1. Online Marketing Tools and Methods

Online marketing has become one of the most lucrative channels for business-to-consumer retailers. This is because consumers tend to spend the majority of their day searching for information, receiving brands, and purchasing goods online. Having a variety of online marketing tools, such as a website, social media, and a blog can help you reach your ideal customers. Here are a few online marketing tools to consider:

- **Social media channels:** One way of selling candles is to advertise the visual appeal. Social media platforms like Instagram and Pinterest can help you curate a feed of stunning photos related to your candle products. Platforms like Facebook are also useful when you desire to build a community brand and share home decor tips or candle guidelines.
- **Email marketing:** A great way to sell directly to customers is to launch an email marketing campaign. In your messages, you can host competitions, give away discounts, or share other brand updates or new product releases.
- **Website:** Your website is the "home" of your brand online. It is usually where you drive potential customers when they click on social media links. You can set up an e-commerce store on your website to appeal to a wider audience. Alternatively, you can share details about your store location or how interested buyers can contact you.

- **Blogs:** Having a blog is a great way to position yourself as a thought leader or expert in the candle-making field. Your articles can include various components of candle-making and lifestyle hacks that your target market may enjoy reading. You can also use articles as a way to promote your products or support an affiliate marketing program.
- **Forums:** If you are looking to create a community, taking part in online forums can help you do just that. Similar to blogs, forums allow you to share information and position yourself as a thought leader. However, the added benefit of joining forums is that they can also be used as a business-to-business networking opportunity.

2. Offline Marketing Tools and Methods

Although online marketing is a great strategy for reaching ideal customers, you shouldn't neglect offline marketing. Many customers prefer to see products like candles in real life before making a purchase. Customers who enjoy visiting home decor or craft stores might also enjoy walking through the aisles and smelling different scented candles as part of their shopping experience. Offline marketing also allows you to get real-time customer feedback about your products. Here are a few tools and methods you can use for offline marketing:

- **Look for wholesale opportunities:** If you are looking to grow your candle-making business, you can approach wholesalers and sell directly to businesses.

You can find wholesalers by contacting chain stores, craft stores, or chatting to vendors at fairs and markets.

- **Create a pop-up shop:** Having a limited-time pop-up shop is a great way to connect with potential customers and introduce your products to them. When people show up at your stall or shop, you can ask them to subscribe to your mailing list or give them a discount code to shop on your website. You can arrange a pop-up display at an already established home decor shop or market. Alternatively, if you live amongst members of your target market, you can set up a table in your front yard and attract people walking by.

- **Network with other business owners:** Another useful offline marketing strategy is to attend workshops, courses, festivals, and other events where you can connect with other candle-making entrepreneurs. Meeting people who are in the same line of work can inspire you with new ideas and help you discover alternative ways of reaching out to customers.

You might decide to invest more time and money in your online marketing than your offline marketing, or vice versa. This is totally fine since your main objective is to appeal to your target market's needs and preferences. For example, if your ideal customer hardly visits markets, it wouldn't be wise for you to sell products at a market. Remember to consider your ideal customer as you put together your marketing strategy, and whether you choose to lean toward the online or offline market, keep these useful tips at the back of your mind:

- **Ensure you take high-quality photos:** High-quality product photos can entice customers to purchase your products. If you can, take photos using a digital camera or good quality smartphone, and ensure the images are clear, bright, and look like they come straight out of a catalog. Use every opportunity to show your label or logo in each photo, so that your brand is recognizable across all marketing platforms.

- **Drive more selling opportunities:** Your goal should be to have repeat customers transacting with your business regularly. To do this, you need to think of ways to bring customers back after they have made their first purchase. Are you going to offer them a discount on their second purchase? Will you run a loyalty program, referral system, or subscription plan? Or are you going to bundle your products so that customers get to sample different products and hopefully come back for more?

- **Broaden your product offerings:** Once you are up and running and have a customer base growing in numbers by the month, consider introducing a new range of candles or adding completely new products to your catalog, like scented soaps or room fresheners, to complement your existing range of candles. When adding a new product, remember to carry out market research, target market analysis, and all the other steps required to identify a market need or gap.

- **Capitalize on holiday sales:** According to the National Candle Association, 35% of candle sales occur during the holiday season, particularly around Christmas time

(National Candle Association, 2018). This means that many shoppers enjoy buying candles as gifts or festive season decorations. To make as many sales during holiday seasons, you will need to prepare in advance by creating a specific candle range and custom scents for the specific holiday and having special promotions and competitions to drive sales.

Now that you have read about creating a USP, take a pen and notebook and list some of your candle's USP.

Continuing with the discussion of selling your candle products, the next chapter will give you more strategies for increasing your number of sales.

15

SELL YOUR PRODUCT

In this chapter, you will learn:

- How to find the proper sales channel to sell your candles.

MAKING THE FIRST SALE

Emma's first customer after incorporating her business wasn't a family friend as she would've hoped. It was a stranger who discovered her Etsy store online as they were browsing through candle products. What was even more exciting is that the stranger lived in a different state and had access to local candle business, but chose to support Emma's online store.

Her second customer was also a stranger, but this time encountered Emma's products at a local market. Since Emma's target market included people who were outgoing and enjoyed social activities, the local market was a great spot to find the ideal buyers. Emma was surprised when the customer bought not one, not two, but three candles because they were going to place them in different rooms around their house.

Now Emma had two lucrative sales channels: Etsy and weekend markets. But these two channels alone wouldn't help her achieve her monthly target sales. She had to explore other channels, such as social media selling and placing some of her products in retail stores. By the end of the first year, Emma was managing a multichannel operation and exceeding her target sales monthly.

CREATING MULTIPLE SALES CHANNELS

Many successful sellers begin with one sales channel but tend to switch to a multi-channel to grow their businesses. While it may seem like a safe option to start with one sales channel, it can restrict the number of sales you make. Since your aim as a business is to be on every platform that your customers engage in, it's important to branch out and sell products on more than one platform too.

For example, selling candles on your e-commerce website is great, but what about also selling on Facebook Marketplace or Etsy if that is where your customers tend to browse for products?

Research by BigCommerce shows that buyers, across all demographics, are shopping on multiple retail channels, both online and offline. A particular survey on American buyers found that buyers often shopped at large retailers (74%), e-commerce marketplaces (54%), web stores (44%), and category-specific online retailers (36%) (Ong, 2018).

There are a few benefits to selling on multiple sales channels. First, you get to appeal to potential customers at different stages of their purchasing journey. The reality is consumers are less likely to purchase your product the first time they encounter your product. They need to be exposed to your product frequently before they are ready to buy. Selling in multiple channels allows you to put your products in buyers' faces as many times as possible, so they are confident in making a purchase.

You can target buyers by listing your products on different platforms, but also having educational content and positive testimonials on your social media pages to increase your brand's credibility. It's also important to ensure that paying customers have an amazing buying experience because word-of-mouth advertising can be a valuable channel to bring in new customers!

Another benefit of multichannel selling is you get to have access to the audience on large e-commerce marketplaces. Online marketplaces like Amazon, Google, Etsy, or Facebook receive an influx of traffic daily. Since they have already built a credible brand and have sophisticated fulfillment processes and return policies, customers would be less hesitant to purchase a product on these marketplaces than an unknown e-commerce store. This doesn't mean that you shouldn't have your own e-commerce store, but you can take advantage of associating your business with reputable e-commerce giants.

How to Create a Multichannel Strategy

Before selling your candle products on multiple channels, you will need to put together a multichannel sales strategy. This will ensure that you do the necessary research and inventory management before you start selling. Here are four elements of an effective multichannel strategy:

1. Know Who You Are Selling To

When you are selling products on multiple channels, you are competing with a greater number of competitors on many factors, including price, quality, and product benefits. However, the more you understand your ideal customer, the more personalized you can make your product offering. For instance, if your customers are after convenience, you can offer a range of payment options, or if your customers are looking for exceptional customer service, they might appreciate free shipping or a flexible return policy. Get to know what your ideal customer's shopping preferences are and try to incorporate these into your sales strategy on each channel.

2. Be Selective When Choosing Your Channels

Placing your products in the wrong channel can cost you money and your reputation. For example, if you list your upmarket candles on a discount website, your customers might doubt whether your candles are worth the price. In general, you should only sell your products on channels that are frequently visited by your customers and are suitable for your brand.

3. Start With One Channel and Build Up

When you launch your candle-making business, start by selling on one channel to get the feel of things. After you have fulfilled a few orders, you can think of the next best channel to extend your business. It's also better to start by selling one product line to test how the market responds to your products. If there are any problems with the product, it will be easy for you to recall products and make the necessary fixes.

4. Manage Your Inventory

There are three things you need to avoid when selling your products: Selling too many products too quickly, running out of stock, and not carefully recording or storing your inventory. To help you manage your inventory, you can purchase inventory management software that can sync across your sales channels and import data about how much inventory has been sold. This will give you plenty of time to order supplies and make sure you always have stock on hand, ready to package and ship to your customers.

Finding the Best Channels for Your Candle-Making Business

You have probably thought about the best places, online and offline, to sell your candles. After all, even though it's good to have a multichannel sales strategy, listing your candles in the wrong channel can be a costly mistake. When choosing a sales channel, it is recommended to go wherever your target market engages the most. For example, if they spend the majority of their time online on Facebook, you can sell your products on Facebook Marketplace. With that being said, you can start with three main sales channels and build up from there. The three main sales channels you should consider are:

1. Online Marketplaces

We have already spoken about the importance of an online marketing strategy; however, an online sales strategy is just as vital. The best way to sell your candles online is through e-commerce websites, including your own. The advantage of selling on your own website is that you get to keep 100% of the profits made from your sales. However, the disadvantage is that you may not receive the same amount of traffic as you would if you listed your products on an e-commerce marketplace. Instead of choosing one or the other, go for both options and sell on your website and marketplaces. Here are a few online marketplaces that can help you sell your products:

- **Etsy:** Etsy is a marketplace that is known for selling handmade and crafted products. This makes it a really good place to sell your handmade candles and appeals to buyers who prefer homemade candles. Nonetheless, this comes at a price. Etsy will charge you a listing fee of $0.20 per product, a 5% transaction fee, and a 3% (plus $0.25) payment processing fee for each transaction.
- **Social media:** While social media is traditionally used for marketing your business, you can also use it for online selling. Platforms like Facebook allow you to create a shop and sell products directly from Facebook or your Etsy and Shopify stores. You can also sell products on Instagram or integrate your Shopify store with Pinterest.

- **Business website:** As mentioned before, you can sell your candles on your very own e-commerce website. To create an e-commerce website, you can design a store on platforms like Shopify or Squarespace. Ensure that your e-commerce website is user-friendly and comes with standard online selling features like a shopping cart, wish list, payment processing integrations, and delivery options.

2. Local Events

If you are a sociable person who enjoys interacting with customers, you can consider selling your products at local events. The advantage of selling face-to-face is that it helps you build rapport with your customers. They can view your products in real-time, ask you questions about the ingredients you used, and give you honest feedback. Here are a few local events that are great for selling candles:

- **Farmer's markets:** Selling at farmer's markets is an affordable way to get in front of your target market. You are likely to come across potential customers who love crafted products and are willing to purchase on the spot. Nevertheless, include marketing material on your stall table so that customers can follow you online.
- **Craft fairs and festivals:** These events occur less frequently than farmer's markets, but they are often bigger in scale and can help you generate a lot of sales. It's important to prepare in advance for craft fairs and festivals by reserving your table many weeks ahead of

time and producing enough candles (and variations of products) to sell on the day or weekend.

3. Wholesaling

Wholesaling involves selling to other businesses, such as retailers, day spas, boutiques, and so on. Businesses would be interested in purchasing large quantities of your candles if their target market demands candles. For instance, have you ever been to a massage parlor that didn't have scented candles in the vicinity? Or visited a home improvement store that didn't have an aisle with rows of candles? Getting started with wholesaling is all about establishing relationships with local business owners. When setting up your meetings, bring along a few candles and any other similar products you produce and pitch your USP.

To get inspiration on creating your own sales channels, study one or two small candle-making businesses that have a presence in at least two sales channels, like an online marketplace and wholesaling, and analyze how they are marketing and selling their products there.

After learning about selling to new consumers via various sales channels, the next step is to ensure a steady stream of sales through repeat customers.

16

SELL. GET POSITIVE REVIEWS. REPEAT

In this chapter, you will learn:

- How to engage with customers to encourage a loyal following which will significantly contribute to your sales growth.

WHAT IS CUSTOMER ENGAGEMENT?

Walt Disney once said, "Do what you do so well that they will want to see it again and bring their friends too" (Bancila, 2015). In this age of technology, customers are bombarded with many options when it comes to products and services. It isn't guaranteed that someone who purchases a product from you once will make a repeat purchase. If there are hundreds of candle businesses, online and offline, which can deliver a candle to a customer's door within a day's notice, what makes them return to a specific store or business?

The secret, as Walt Disney understood, is having a customer-centric business that puts a lot of effort into taking care of customers. Each time a customer purchases a candle from your business, there are about three other candle businesses they turned down. To ensure that they continue to support your business, you need to give them a reason to keep coming back.

Many start-up businesses mistakenly believe that offering the lowest prices is the best way to ensure customers' returns. However, this isn't always the case. While price is an important factor in making a purchasing decision, a customer will also consider the shopping experience and customer service they experience with certain businesses. If a customer is treated well, they won't mind paying a few extra dollars for a product or service. In other words, the customer service experience increases the perceived value of the product or service. However, if they are treated poorly, they will go through the hassle of contacting other businesses the next time they need a similar product.

As a small business owner, your mission will be to bring new customers and turn them into repeat customers. You can do this by improving your customer engagement. Customer engagement is the process of building meaningful relationships with the customers you serve. It involves the entire journey you walk with customers from your first encounter online or over the phone to the exchange of emails you have after each successful sale. There are many opportunities you can take advantage of before, during, and after a sale that can help you connect to your customers and ensure that your business stays at the top of their minds.

Customer engagement requires a solid strategy of how you will communicate with your customers at various stages of the buying process. You can't simply rely on the information about your target market since this kind of engagement needs you to interact on a one-on-one basis with each customer. You will need to think about the best channels to interact with your customers, how to contact them, and which communication tools can increase customer satisfaction.

How to Create a Customer Engagement Strategy

A customer engagement strategy can improve your customer relations and positively impact your brand's reputation. It can increase the likelihood of repeat customers and customers referring your candle-making business to friends and family. Word-of-mouth advertising and positive online reviews can be a multiplier of success for small businesses. Below are three tips to use when creating your customer engagement strategy:

1. Set a Goal

Think about the kind of relationships you desire to have with your customers. For instance, do you want to be the expert your customers turn to when they need candle inspiration or home decorating tips? Do you want them to purchase your candles monthly, seasonally, or whenever they throw a party? And do you want your customers to have direct access to you as the owner or to go through an employee? The kind of relationship you desire with your customers will help you set goals for your customer engagement. You will know the kind of language to use in your marketing material, the kinds of call-to-actions that will be effective, and how to follow up with your customer after each purchase.

2. Create Short and Long-Term Tactics

Ideally, you want to build long-term relationships with each customer and be a part of their lives for many years to come. However, your customer engagement strategy must be broken down into short and long-term tactics that can be used to help you focus on the right communication tools and methods for each stage of the customer journey. For example, when a potential customer is still deciding whether to purchase one of your products or not, they will want to make frequent contact with you to ask you questions. However, after the fifth purchase, the same customer may not need to hear from you as much. Therefore, you need to assess the kind of communication needs and preferences your customers will have before, during, and after making a purchase, and create short and long-term tactics accordingly.

3. Gather Feedback and Continuously Adjust Your Customer Engagement Strategy

The best way to determine if your customer engagement strategy works is to ask for feedback from your customers. They can tell you what they like or dislike about engaging with your business. Take time to review your strategy quarterly to ensure you are achieving the goals you set out and are making your customers happy. Adjust your strategy according to your customers' needs, and continue to ask for feedback.

Customer Engagement Tactics

Based on your customer engagement strategy, you will be able to create a list of tactics to employ so you can build relationships with your customers. Here are a few tactics that may work for your business:

1. Establish Your Brand Voice

Customers want to feel as though they are interacting with a personality when they engage with your business. Establishing your brand voice is one way to distinguish your brand from other candle brands in the market. Try to imagine how your brand would sound or behave if it were a real person. This will help you create a unique brand voice that will inform how you communicate with your customers.

2. Share Relevant Content

If you want to reach out to the right customers, you must design content that will appeal to them. Avoid making generic content that would attract a wide audience, since this kind of content is saturated online. Instead, be intentional about what you post and where you post it, so you can excite your ideal buyers.

3. Create Brand Advocates

Brand advocates are customers who are so thrilled to support your business that they share your posts, tag your brand in their captions, and cannot stop singing your praises. Customers are usually willing to become brand advocates when they see your brand as being more than a business. For them, your brand offers a lifestyle, community, or opportunity to improve their lives. Think of ways of being more than a business to your customers, such as showing your support, remembering their birthdays or other important milestones, or following your customers on social media. Show them that you are just as interested in their lives as they are in your business.

4. Publicize Your Reviews

Whenever you receive a positive review from a customer, post it up on your social media pages and website and build a positive reputation for your brand. Potential customers want to know what to expect when doing business with you to reduce as much risk in the buying process. When they see real people sharing positive experiences about your business, they can feel less hesitant to follow through with a purchase.

5. Deliver on Your Promises

The quickest way businesses discredit themselves is by not keeping their promises, especially their USP. This is especially true for small businesses that only get one chance to make a good impression on a customer. Go through your marketing content and copy and identify promises that you make to customers. This could be promising next day delivery, friendly customer service, or 30-day money-back guarantee. Think long and hard about each promise and whether you have the capacity (time, money, and labor) to fulfill them. Cross out any promises you are not yet ready to make and do everything in your power to fulfill the rest.

After building a customer following and positively increasing your sales, the next step is to automate your business processes and run your business on autopilot.

PART VI

KEEP THE FLAME ALIVE:

RUNNING ON AUTOPILOT FOR EFFICIENCY

17

AUTOMATING YOUR BUSINESS AND PROCESSES

In this chapter, you will learn:

- How to use various tools to streamline several business aspects, such as the process of making candles, accounting, and customer engagement.

PUT YOUR BUSINESS ON AUTOPILOT

Two years after launching her candle-making business, Emma's business thrived, despite the quarantine. She was able to hit a six-figure revenue and distribute her candles to around 20 stores in her area. Instead of manually visiting each store and checking how many sales she has made, Emma uses software that keeps track of her sales in each of her sales channels. Emma has also been able to build a tribe of customers, both online and offline, which she regularly contacts through scheduled email campaigns. All of this growth wouldn't be possible if

Emma didn't decide to automate some of her business systems to save time and money.

WHAT IS BUSINESS AUTOMATION?

In the first year or two of running your business, you will be hands-on. You may not have enough sales or cash to justify having employees, so you will handle most of your business tasks on your own. However, as your sales increase and each aspect of your business becomes more demanding of your time, you will need to decide whether to hire someone or automate specific processes.

Automating business processes is the alternative to doing things manually. Instead of assigning a task to yourself or an employee, you allow a software program or app to do the task for you. This can save you time and money, it can also improve the speed of your business operations. For example, think about how long it would take you to send 100 emails each day to potential customers, as compared to creating one template, pushing the "send" button, and letting your emailing service do the rest.

Automating your business won't replace the need for employees because some tasks still require human efforts, such as picking up calls, creating personalized emails to customers, and responding to social media and other business inquiries. You will also need a human to produce and package your candles, as well as handle your deliveries. However, for other tasks, such as combining your candle ingredients, doing administrative work, or scheduling marketing content, you can use technology. Below are examples of how to automate specific aspects of your candle-making business:

- **Have a chatbot on your website.** Having a self-service tool, like a chatbot, can ensure visitors receive the support they need after hours or when you are unable to respond to inquiries right away.
- **Manage several business processes on one software or platform.** To improve workflow and efficiency, you can manage several different processes, like customer relations, shipping and deliveries, and inventory management, on one platform that allows you to integrate several task management apps.
- **Generate statistics, reports, and financial statements on a reporting tool.** Reporting tools allow you to upload data (or you can give them data permission) and they can calculate, measure, and create assessments and reports based on the data provided.
- **Automate your social media scheduling.** Instead of manually posting social media content every few days, you can create a calendar and schedule different types of content to feature on different social media platforms, on specific days and at specific times. You can also view reports and statistics of your social media engagement through a social media reporting tool.

A good rule of thumb when deciding which tasks to automate is to look for repetitive tasks, don't require a lot of human effort, and slow down your workflow. These are generally tasks that can be automated without compromising the integrity of your business.

USING MACHINES TO AUTOMATE THE CANDLE-MAKING PROCESS

When you are receiving large orders and cannot physically produce that many candles on your own, you can invest in a candle-making machine. A candle-making machine can produce candles of any size, in large quantities, while also reducing as much wax waste as possible.

Using a candle-making machine can save you time and improve the quality and uniformity of your candles. When picking a machine, you have the option of choosing between three types of machines:

- **Manual candle-making machines:** These types of machines can help you solidify wax into molds and can produce between 300-950 candles per hour, depending on the size of the machine.
- **Semi-automatic candle-making machines:** All you need to do when operating these machines is adjust the settings and it will take care of the dimensions, cooling, and other aspects of the candle-making process.
- **Automatic candle-making machines:** These are the most advanced types of candle-making machines that come with many features and the ability to make scented, colorful, and different shaped candles, with

accurate dimensions. A standard automatic machine can produce about 240 candles per minute.

In addition to business processes, you can also automate your marketing and social media engagement to free you up from a lot of tasks.

18

AUTOMATING YOUR COMPANY'S MARKETING AND CUSTOMER ENGAGEMENT

In this chapter, you will learn:

- How to run your business on autopilot, this time touching on marketing and customer engagement.

AUTOMATE YOUR MARKETING AND CUSTOMER ENGAGEMENT TASKS

The benefit of growing your business is that you don't need to wear as many hats anymore. If software or online tools can do the job better than you, you can hand over some of your business tasks. One of the key areas of a business that require expertise is marketing and customer engagement. Even though you can't automate these areas completely, you can look for small, repetitive tasks to save yourself time. Here are a few examples of ways to automate your marketing and customer engagement tasks:

- **Scheduling social media content.** As discussed in the previous chapter, you can save time by creating your content in advance and using scheduling tools to automate when your content goes live. These scheduling tools also allow you to manage several social media accounts all in one calendar and keep your content organized.

- **Using a website builder.** Once again, you can save yourself time and money by designing your website using a website builder, rather than getting a website developer to create your site. Website builders normally include hundreds of professional templates that can be customized according to your type of business.

- **Run automated surveys.** You need customer feedback to improve customer engagement. However, manually creating a survey each time you seek feedback can be time-consuming. You can create automated review or feedback forms that are sent via email or through your website after a customer has made a purchase. To incentivize completing the survey, you can offer customers a special discount code.

- **Create automated customer reminders.** There are digital tools that can remind customers to complete their purchase on your e-commerce site or remind them about an upcoming sale. Customers can also receive emails to sign up for special newsletters, subscription plans, and courses or workshops. You can also set a reminder to email a customer when you haven't heard from them in a while.

- **Use mobile marketing.** An often overlooked marketing channel is mobile marketing. According to Reviews.org, Americans check their cell phones 344 times per day, which is about once every 4 minutes (Wheelwright, 2020). Since your customers are more than likely always on their phones, you can engage with them through push notifications on a mobile app, or create a group on a messaging platform like WhatsApp.

After covering both the creative and business aspects of your candle-making business, the next chapters are dedicated to providing answers or advice about the candle-making business.

PART VII

FAQS AND ADDITIONAL TIPS

19

CANDLE-MAKING FAQS

In this chapter, you will learn:

- Other aspects of the candle-making business that might not have been covered or detailed in the previous chapters.

YOUR CANDLE-MAKING QUESTIONS ANSWERED!

So far, we have already covered as much ground as possible about candle-making. This chapter addresses some of the most common questions aspiring entrepreneurs have about the candle-making business and may present a condensed version of the discussions in the previous chapters.

Q: How do you pick the right wick size?

A: If it is your first time making candles, determining the appropriate wick size can be tricky. Fortunately, you can refer to the wick chart that has been developed by CandleScience to determine the right type and size of wick for different types of containers.

Q: Where do you buy candle supplies?

A: It's important to have a list of suppliers you can contact so you have more options of supplies to choose from—and can compare prices to get the best offer. If possible, start your search by looking for local suppliers. You can save a lot of money on shipping costs by simply driving a few miles to collect your supplies, or better yet, have them delivered to your home. If you can't find any candle supply stores, look for craft or home decor stores. Alternatively, you can always shop for your candle supplies online on sites like Amazon and Candle-Science.

Q: How can you prevent candle imperfections caused by soy wax?

A: Since soy wax is polymorphic, meaning it can react in unpredictable ways and cause performance problems. The best way to prevent as many imperfections as possible is to manage your pour temperature, ensure that you mix your fragrances evenly, and allow your wax candle to cure for an appropriate amount of time.

Q: How many candles should you make when starting?

A: The choice is up to you on how many candles you would like to produce. Some candle-makers have a vast product range, with different colored and scented candles, while others have a product range consisting of 2-3 types of colored or scented candles. The only thing to remember is that you must cater to the needs of your market. If there isn't a high demand for your products, don't make too many candles, otherwise, you will be left with a lot of inventory that never sells.

Q: How do you improve your hot throw?

A: Hot throw is the scent emitted when a candle is burning. To test how strong your candle scent is, burn a candle in a room (preferably the bathroom) for four hours. Check on your candle every hour and rate the intensity of the scent on a scale of 1— 10 (1 being weak and 10 being very strong). Once you have gathered the results, burn the same candle in a larger room like the living room and conduct the same test.

Q: How can you make a candle-making business successful?

A: While many factors contribute to the success of a business, understanding your target market, especially your ideal customer, can help you define your brand and market your products in a manner that appeals to them. It's also helpful to know which channels to find your ideal customers so you can ensure they are exposed to your products.

Q: Do you need a business license to sell homemade candles?

A: If you intend on producing candles for resale then you will need to have a business license to sell your products. For example, before a wholesaler accepts your products in their store, they will ask for legal documents to see if you have incorporated your business. Online customers who buy from your website may also want to see proof of your business license and other documents proving you are a credible business.

Q: What happens if you overheat your wax?

A: Generally, when you overheat your wax, it causes discoloration, a poor scent throw, and a weakened end product. In most cases, the best option is to start the heating process all over again.

Q: How much money can you make from a candle-making business?

A: Each candle-making business's revenue will range depending on several factors; however, statistics show that at the entry-level, a candle-making business can make around $22,000 a year (excluding rent, labor costs, and manufacturing costs).

Q: Do you need insurance to run a candle-making business?

A: If you are running an LLC, your assets will be protected against any business liability. However, you will still need to take out product liability insurance to protect your business against any claims or lawsuits on the products you produce and sell. If you have employees, you can also take out employee unemployment cover and insurance to cover medical bills for accidental injuries on the job.

Now that we have some of the common questions out of the way, the next chapter will provide additional tips to make your first year running a candle-making business as smooth as possible.

ADDITIONAL TIPS TO GET YOU ON YOUR WAY

In this chapter, you will learn:

- Other ways to grow and sustain your candle-making business, including scaling it up or diversifying your business.

BUILD YOUR TEAM

The final chapter of the book is aimed at entrepreneurs who want to step up their game in the candle-making business and ensure sustained growth. The first way to do this is to bring on board a team of dedicated employees. Please note that this will only be necessary once your sales increase to the point where you need more assistance in running your business. Until then, automating some business tasks will be sufficient!

So, what kind of roles would you need to fill for your unique business? Here is a list of the basic positions you can fill as you create your dream team:

1. Candle-maker
2. Label producer
3. Candle packer and delivery man/woman
4. Marketing strategist and content maker
5. IT specialist (to manage your e-commerce website)
6. Accountant

Depending on the scale of your operations, you may need to hire more than one of these professionals for each role, like having three candle-makers. Cost-effective ways of recruiting employees is to create a free job vacancy post on job sites like LinkedIn or Facebook. Alternatively, you can pay a small premium on sites like Glassdoor or Indeed and advertise your job posting to a wider audience. You can also ask your friends and family if they know of anyone looking for contract work.

SELL YOUR BRAND STORY

A brand story tells potential customers who you are, why you exist, and where you envision yourself in a few years. It can help people connect to your brand, especially if they can relate to your story. From your story, you can create your brand culture, voice, and message, which informs how you market and run your business, both online and offline. It is a lot easier for customers to recite your brand story than it is for them to remember specific products that you sell. Remember that a good brand story is always captivating, causes customers to feel something, and as a result, drives them to take action.

There are a few questions you can ask yourself when coming up with your brand story. These include:

- Why did I enter the candle-making business?
- Who am I making candles for?
- What impact do I want my business to have on the customers I serve?
- What impact do I want to make in the candle-making industry?

IDENTIFY YOUR BUSY SEASONS AND BEST SCENTS

Two things can boost your revenue: Capitalizing on busy seasons and finding the perfect scents to sell to customers. There are many opportunities throughout the year to sell candles. Of course, the busy seasons are often around holiday time.

Nevertheless, this doesn't mean that you can't make sales during low seasons. A great way to boost your sales in low seasons is to sell seasonal scents. Customers purchase seasonal scented candles because they complement the smells, colors, and ambience around the home or during special occasions. Here is an example of a few seasonal scents to consider:

Spring Scents

- Cherry blossom

- Apple blossom
- Honeysuckle
- Lavender
- Jasmine
- Lemongrass
- Lilac
- Lilies
- Magnolias

Summer Scents

- Sea salt
- Ocean
- Citrus
- Wine
- Sandalwood
- Peaches
- Watermelon
- Citronella
- Aloe
- Linen

Fall

- Cinnamon
- Apple
- Pumpkin spice
- Eucalyptus
- Sage
- Tobacco

- Brown sugar
- Cedar

Winter

- Vanilla
- Cinnamon
- Pine
- Orchid
- Peppermint
- Maple
- Chestnut
- Nutmeg
- Juniper
- Birch

Besides showing your versatility with the different scents you offer, you can generate more revenue during your low seasons by following these marketing tips:

- Give away discounts to your emailing list
- Run a competition
- Research obscure holidays and find a way to create fun candles in honor of them (these candles don't need to be for sale, they can simply be used for marketing content).

CONCLUSION

Throughout the book, we have been inspired by Emma's entrepreneurial journey into making and selling candles. Like any other passionate entrepreneur, she started her business hoping for the best, not realizing that she would face many challenges along the way. Nonetheless, she showed resilience during difficult moments and the results speak for themselves.

Unlike Emma, you are fortunate enough to have access to information about candles and candle-making from two industry experts. The techniques and advice you have received from this book will ensure you avoid as many risks along your candle-making journey. Of course, if you ever feel stuck or need a little bit of moral support, you can turn to online forums and communities where you can interact with other candle-makers like yourself.

The candle-making business is thriving and there is no better time than now to enter the industry and find your gap in the market. Even though candles use similar materials, like wax and wicks, there are plenty of variations of candles you can make and specific market segments you can sell your candles to. And if your local area is already crowded with candle stores, you have the freedom and flexibility to branch out and sell online to a broader audience.

So, what do you need to get started?

Having a decent workspace at home, as well as a few old pots, a few chunks of wax, and wicks can help you kick-start your business. This is all you will need to practice making candles. The rest of the tools and equipment you can purchase as you master making candles and are confident enough to sell them for cash.

Once again, you have plenty of options when it comes to choosing your target market and your ideal customers. You can make your market as niche or large as you want, although remember to price your candles according to what your type of customer is willing to pay. If you haven't yet chosen the right pricing strategy, you can refer back to chapter 11 and have another read!

Marketing your candle-making business is another area where you can get creative. You can pick between online or offline marketing—or better yet—go for both! In the game of marketing, there isn't such a thing as "too much exposure" if you are marketing to the right customers, on the right marketing channels. Trust me, your ideal customers won't get tired of seeing your promotional content or hearing about your newest product launches.

Bear in mind, that a marketing channel isn't necessarily an appropriate sales channel. Your marketing channels will help you advertise your brand and get the word out about your products, but your sales channels are where you will direct your customers so they can purchase your products. There are times when a marketing channel can serve as a sales channel too, such as marketing and selling products on social media. Although, the main aim of sales channels in most cases is to sell products (some examples include Etsy, Amazon, and your personal website).

As you grow your candle-making business, keep in mind that your goal is to turn potential customers into repeat customers. You want customers who start as suspicious strangers to end up being brand advocates who journey with you for many years. Treating your customers well and finding ways to continue the conversation throughout the purchasing journey is how you can have them coming back to purchase more candles.

Your customers probably won't remember the price they paid for their candles or which scents were their favorite, but they will certainly remember the shopping experience and convenience of engaging with your business. Treat each customer like they are your first and last customer, and make their experience buying candles from you memorable.

After all of the planning, strategizing, and executing of your tasks, all that's left is to automate your business processes and watch as your sales grow. Even though you will probably reach this stage after the first year of juggling many hats and managing most of your business tasks on your own, it is certainly worth the wait.

Automating your process allows you to step back as the business owner and prioritize your time on key areas of your business. The rest of the admin and repetitive tasks are handled by an AI bot. Nevertheless, AI bots haven't reached the point where they can answer calls and write personalized emails to customers. So you will probably need a dedicated customer service team who can help you with more human tasks.

Now that you have been given the necessary skills and knowledge to start your candle-making business, the only thing left for you to do is commit to start NOW. If there is ever a time when you need guidance, you can refer back to this book, or pose a question on a candle-making Facebook group.

Remember that candle-making is naturally a creative business. Try not to get too bogged down by the legal and administrative aspects of your business that you forget to have some fun, play around with colors, and be innovative.

If this is a passion project, take as much time as you need to get it off the ground, but if this is a profit-driven business venture, the market is ready and waiting for your range of candles (and the many variations of products that will come as you scale your business).

Don't fret about making your business profitable. As long as you handle the various aspects of your business that we have discussed, your candle-making business can become as successful as you want it to be. Truly, the sky's the limit for you!

So, unleash your creativity and bring something new to the market. We are all waiting with bated breath to witness the success of your start-up business!

If you have found this book useful, please leave a review and share your candle-making experience!

GLOSSARY

Beeswax: Substance created by the worker bees and processed to remove all impurities left from the comb.

Burn rate: The ease at which solid wax liquifies when placed under a heat source, such as a flame from a wick. Candle-makers also refer to burn time, which is the amount of time it normally takes for a wax candle to burn completely.

Coconut wax: A wax product made from coconut meat and hydrogenated to increase its melting point and maintain a solid consistency under normal room temperatures.

Cold throw: The strength of a candle's scent when it is not lit.

Container candle: A candle that is poured into a container and allowed to set until the time it is burned.

Cure: The process of allowing a candle to harden and secure the dye and fragrance.

Double boiler: Two pans that come as one set. Water is often added to the lower pan and brought to the boil, so that the content inside the top pan is heated evenly and slowly.

Dye: Various colorants that are used to give wax color.

Essential oils: Natural oils sourced from a variety of plants and herbs.

Hot throw: The strength of a candle's scent when it is lit.

Melt point: The temperature at which solid wax begins to liquify.

Melt pool: The amount of liquid wax that forms in a candle as it is burning. The melt pool is often characterized by its depth or diameter.

Molds: Aluminum casings that are used to set a candle when making pillar candles.

Mushrooming: When carbon builds up at the tip of a wick after burning, causing a black stain. This phenomenon usually happens when the wick is too short for the candle size

Paraffin wax: A type of non-renewable wax made from petroleum and used for making a variety of candles.

Pillar candles: A freestanding candle that is set using a mold.

Pour temperature: The temperature to pour melted wax into a container or mold casing.

Primed wick: A wick that is prepared for candle-making by coating it in multiple layers of wax before leaving it to dry.

Re-pour: The process of filling the space left after the wax has been left to cool so that the top of the candle can be leveled.

Scent load: The amount of fragrance a wax can hold (typically stated in percentage value).

Scent throw: The amount of fragrance emitted by a candle (it can be light or strong).

Soy wax: A natural type of wax made from soybean oil.

Synthetic oils/fragrances: Factory-produced oils and fragrances.

Taper candle: A freestanding candle that becomes thinner the closer it gets to the wick. These types of candles usually come with candle holders to ensure stability.

Tunneling: When the candle burns right down the middle instead of creating an even melt pool. This phenomenon is caused by the wick being too small for the candle size.

Votive candle: A relatively small candle that is burned in a votive container.

REFERENCES

Amaresan, S. (2021). The Ultimate Guide to Customer Engagement in 2020. Blog.hubspot.com. https://blog.hubspot.com/service/customer-engagement-guide

Australian Government. (2021, August). Identify your target market. Business.gov.au. https://business.gov.au/marketing/identify-your-target-market

Bancila, A. (2015, July). Do what you do so well that they will want to see it again and bring their friends too. Www.translationdirectory.com. https://www.translationdirectory.com/articles/article2519.php

CandleScience. (n.d.-a). Choosing the Right Wick Size - Candle Making Guide. CandleScience - Candle and Soap Making Supplies. https://www.candlescience.com/learning/choosing-the-right-wick-size/

CandleScience. (n.d.-b). Starting Your Own Candle Making Business: A Blueprint for Success. CandleScience - Candle and Soap Making Supplies. https://www.candlescience.com/starting-your-own-candle-business-a-blueprint-for-success/

CandleScience. (n.d.-c). Where to Sell Your Candles: Finding the Right Channel. CandleScience - Candle and Soap Making Supplies. https://www.candlescience.com/where-to-sell-your-candles-finding-the-right-channel/

Carbajo, M. (2018, July 18). Choosing the Right Business Structure: Three Factors to Consider. Choosing the Right Business Structure: Three Factors to Consider. https://www.sba.gov/blog/choosing-right-business-structure-three-factors-consider

CB Insights. (2019, March 15). The Top 20 Reasons Startups Fail. CB Insights Research. https://www.cbinsights.com/research/startup-failure-reasons-top/

Checkify Blog. (n.d.). Why Automate Business Processes? Checkify. https://checkify.com/blog/why-automate-business-processes/

Creative Candles. (2020, January 1). A History of Candle Use. Creative Candles. https://creativecandles.com/blogs/inspiration/a-history-of-candle-use

Customer Service. (2020, March 25). How to Make Pillar Candles. Candlewic. https://candlewic.com/learn/candlemaking-how-to/how-to-make-pillar-candles/

DeMarco, J. (2020, October 22). How to Start a Candle Business. NerdWallet. https://www.nerdwallet.com/article/small-business/how-to-start-a-candle-business

Elizabeth. (2020, February 1). What is Candle Wax Made of? Your Guide to Types of Wax. Osmology; Osmology. https://www.osmology.co/blog/which-wax/

Finn, J. (2012, August 20). How-to: Hand-Dipped Wax Candles. Crafting a Green World. https://craftingagreenworld.com/articles/how-to-hand-dipped-wax-candles/

Fischer, K. (2020a, March 24). 7 Ways to Clean Up Your Workstation. Armatage Candle Company. https://armatagecandlecompany.com/blog/candle-makers-cleaning-guide-7-ways-to-clean-up-your-workstation/

Fischer, K. (2020b, August 14). 5 Strategies to Stick Out In A Saturated Candle Market. Armatage Candle Company. https://armatagecandlecompany.com/blog/stick-out-in-a-saturated-candle-market/

Fischer, K. (2020c, November 7). 10 Common Candle Making Questions. Armatage Candle Company. https://armatagecandlecompany.com/blog/candle-making-questions/

Fisher, D. (2020a, January 16). Different Types of Handmade Candles. The Spruce Crafts. https://www.thesprucecrafts.com/types-of-handmade-candles-516769

Fisher, D. (2020b, July 8). Make a Simple Rolled Beeswax Candle. The Spruce Crafts. https://www.thesprucecrafts.com/rolled-beeswax-candles-517038

Frontier Label. (2021, October 14). How and Why to Start Your Own Candle Business + TONS of Resources. Frontier Label. https://www.frontierlabel.com/blog/how-and-why-to-start-your-own-candle-business-tons-of-resources

Funk, L. (2017, November 20). 5 Ways Marketing Automation Makes Engagement Easy. Marketo Marketing Blog - Best Practices and Thought Leadership; Marketo. https://blog.marketo.com/2017/11/5-ways-marketing-automation-makes-engagement-easy.html

Ganassini, M. G. (2016, December 28). 60 (+1) Digital Marketing Quotes to Inspire Your Strategies. MailUp Blog. https://blog.mailup.com/2016/12/digital-marketing-quotes/

Glassnow. (2019, April 15). 10 Candle Business Marketing Tips. Glassnow. https://www.glassnow.com/blog/10-candle-business-marketing-tips/ #Promote_Your_Candle_Business_Online_-_The_Good_Stuff

Global Alliance of SMEs. (n.d.). Types of Business Entities & Corporation in the USA. Www.globalsmes.org. http://www.globalsmes.org/news/index. php?func=detail&detailid=417&catalog=22&lan=en&search_keywords=

Goodreads. (2019). *A quote by Benjamin Franklin*. Goodreads.com. https:// www.goodreads.com/quotes/460142-if-you-fail-to-plan-you-are-plan ning-to-fail

IBISWorld. (2020, October 28). IBISWorld - Industry Market Research, Reports, and Statistics. Www.ibisworld.com. https://www.ibisworld.com/ industry-statistics/market-size/candle-manufacturing-united-states/

Idea2MakeMoney. (2017, September 8). Candle Making Business - A Beginners Guide. Www.idea2makemoney.com. https://www.idea2makemoney. com/candle-making-business-beginners-guide

Jurgaityte, G. (2018, June 26). 7 Tips on How to Manage Multiple Sales Channels. https://multiorders.com/7-tips-on-how-to-manage-multiple-sales-channels/

Katsis, F. (2016, April 25). Setting Up Your Candle Making Workspace. Soycandles.melbourne. https://soycandles.melbourne/2016/04/25/ setting-up-your-candle-making-workspace/

Keenan, M. (2021, April 13). Turn Scents Into Dollars: How to Start a Candle-Making Business (Plus Examples From Top-Selling Candle Brands). Shopify. https://www.shopify.com/ph/blog/candle-business#13

Kirsty. (2020, May 9). What are the different types of candle wax? Rowbert. https://www.rowbert.com/post/what-are-the-different-types-of-candle-wax

Larkin, K. Y. (n.d.). Candle Making Business Budget. LoveToKnow. https:// candles.lovetoknow.com/Candle_Making_Business_Budget

Leon, J. N. (2019, June 11). 4 Easy Steps to Understand The Fail of "No Market Need". Start-ups Tips. https://startupstips.com/4-easy-steps-to-understand-the-no-market-need/

Lit Up Candle Co. (2018, April 17). 10 WAYS YOU'LL BENEFIT FROM BURNING CANDLES. Lit up Candle Co. https://litupcandleco.com/ blogs/get-lit/benefits-from-burning-candles

Maldonaldo, Z. (2020, July 20). 5 Ways to Reduce Small Business Startup

Costs. Bplans Blog. https://articles.bplans.com/4-creative-ways-to-reduce-small-business-startup-costs/

Miller, S. (2021, September 24). How to Make Candles at Home - An Easy guide. Workshopedia. https://workshopedia.com/how-to-make-candles-at-home-an-easy-guide/

Mondloch, R. (2020, October 24). 5 Candle Making Safety Tips Everyone Should Follow. NorthWood Distributing. https://northwoodcandlesupply.com/blogs/news/5-candle-making-safety-tips-everyone-should-follow

National Candle Association. (2014a). Elements of a Candle: Colorants. National Candle Association. https://candles.org/elements-of-a-candle/colorants/

National Candle Association. (2014b). Elements of a Candle: Fragrance. National Candle Association. https://candles.org/elements-of-a-candle/fragrance/

National Candle Association. (2018). Facts& Figures. National Candle Association. https://candles.org/facts-figures-2/

National Candle Association. (2020). Home. National Candle Association. https://candles.org/

Neff, M. (2020, October 27). How to Brand Your Candle Line. Avery. https://www.avery.com/blog/how-to-brand-your-candle-line/

Ong, A. (2018, August 13). Multi-Channel Retailing and the Buyer's Journey: Opportunities and Challenges. The BigCommerce Blog. https://www.bigcommerce.com/blog/multi-channel-retailing/#multi-channel-product-information-management

Orosz, D. (2021, October 29). How to Start a Candle Business. Step by Step Business. https://stepbystepbusiness.com/business-ideas/start-a-candle-business/

Philosiblog. (2013, August 20). Thousands of candles can be lit from a single one, and its life will not be shortened. Happiness never decreases by being shared. Philosiblog. https://philosiblog.com/2013/08/20/thousands-of-candles-can-be-lit-from-a-single-one-and-its-life-will-not-be-shortened-happiness-never-decreases-by-being-shared/

Sheehan, A. (2020, October 25).Six Things To Consider Before You Commit To a Wholesale Candle Supplier. Handshake Blog. https://blog.handshake.com/wholesale-candle-suppliers/

Shewan, D. (2021, November 22). How to Write a Ferociously Unique Selling

Proposition. Wordstream.com. https://www.wordstream.com/blog/ws/2014/04/07/unique-selling-proposition

Starter Story. (n.d.). 35 Pros and Cons of Starting a Candle Business. Www.starterstory.com. https://www.starterstory.com/ideas/candle-business/pros-and-cons

Starting Your Business. (2021, September 15). What Licenses Does a Candle Making Business Need? Startingyourbusiness.com. https://startingyourbusiness.com/what-licenses-does-a-candle-making-business-need/

The Curiously Creative. (2019, April 27). The Ultimate Guide to Candle Making for Beginners. The Curiously Creative. https://www.thecuriouslycreative.com/candle-making-for-beginners/

ThriveHive. (2018, February 5). What to Know About Your Target Market. ThriveHive. https://thrivehive.com/what-to-know-about-your-target-market/

Tight Fist Finance. (2021, February 1). Make money selling candles from home. TightFist Finance. https://tightfistfinance.com/make-money-selling-candles-from-home/

Trounce, D. (2021, September 21). 7 Ways to Put Your Online Business on Autopilot. GrowMap. https://growmap.com/online-business-on-autopilot/

Unleashed. (n.d.). Your Guide to Effective Multichannel Selling. Unleashed Software. https://www.unleashedsoftware.com/inventory-management-guide/your-guide-to-multichannel-selling

Verified Market Research. (2022, February). *Candle Market Size, Share, Trends, Opportunities and Forecast.* Verified Market Research. https://www.verifiedmarketresearch.com/product/candle-market/

Vogel, K. (2020, October 12). 10 Customer engagement strategies from real small businesses. RingCentral. https://www.ringcentral.com/us/en/blog/customer-engagement-strategies/

Vojinovic, I. (2022, February 4).50+ Eye-Opening Branding Statistics - 2022 Edition. SmallBizGenius. https://www.smallbizgenius.net/by-the-numbers/branding-statistics/#gref

WaxMelters. (n.d.). Candle Business & Industry Facts. Www.waxmelters.com. https://www.waxmelters.com/Candle-Business-Industry-Facts-s/54.htm

Wheelwright, T. (2020, February 11). 2022 Cell Phone Usage Statistics: How Obsessed Are We? Reviews.org. https://www.reviews.org/mobile/cell-phone-addiction/

Yelp. (2020a, December 2). 9 Types of pricing strategies to meet your business goals. Yelp for Business. https://business.yelp.com/grow/types-of-pricing-strategies/

Yelp. (2020b, December 2). 9 Types of pricing strategies to meet your business goals. Yelp for Business. https://business.yelp.com/grow/types-of-pricing-strategies/

Yoco Editor. (2021, April 28). How to write a concise funding proposal for your small business. Open by Yoco. https://www.yoco.com/za/blog/article/concise-funding-proposal-writing/

Young Entrepreneur Council. (2018, December 12). Top Eight Tips For Finding Startup Funding. Forbes. https://www.forbes.com/sites/theyec/2018/12/12/top-eight-tips-for-finding-startup-funding/